These Earthen Vessels

The Christian and His Failures,
Foibles, and Infirmities

To Mrs. Schofield
with many thanks & much
appreciation for our happy
memories of England.

Helen Temple

These Earthen Vessels

The Christian and His Failures, Foibles, and Infirmities

by

W. T. Purkiser, Ph.D.

Beacon Hill Press of Kansas City
Kansas City, Missouri

Unless otherwise indicated, all Scripture quotations are from *The Holy Bible, New International Version,* copyright © 1978 by the New York International Bible Society, and are used by permission of Zondervan Bible Publishers.

Permission to quote from other copyrighted versions of the Bible is acknowledged with appreciation as follows:

The Bible: A New Translation (Moffatt), copyright 1954 by James A. R. Moffatt. By permission of Harper and Row, Publishers, Inc.

New Testament in Modern English (Phillips), Revised Edition © J. B. Phillips, 1958, 1960, 1972. By permission of the Macmillan Publishing Co.

Revised Standard Version of the Bible (RSV), copyrighted 1946, 1952, © 1971, 1973.

10 9 8 7 6 5 4 3 2 1

CONTENTS

PREFACE

The material on the following pages was prepared in connection with a series of messages delivered at the Southern California District Holiness Crusade and Camp Meeting at Point Loma Nazarene College in San Diego, July 30 to August 5, 1984, as the first of a projected "W. T. Purkiser Holiness Lecture Series." It relates to a topic that is of vital importance in understanding the Wesleyan concept of Christian holiness.

We really must admit that we have not always come to terms with human failures and foibles, weakness, ignorance, immaturity, and infirmities. The result has been a growing "credibility gap" in an age increasingly concerned with practical outcomes.

Not much of the material here is new. Some of it has been used in other contexts. Any distinction it has lies in the bringing together of ideas and insights from a number of varied sources. There are some relevant topics that are not treated. Some that are discussed deserve more space than could be given.

As will be pointed out in context later, the New Testament passage around which the material is organized (2 Cor. 4:7-18) is used in an adapted sense. The fascinating relevance of the New Testament Epistles lies in the fact that they treat local and often temporary situations in the light of eternal principles, which are always timely because they are timeless.

The Corinthian correspondence is a particularly good example of this feature of the New Testament. The Corinthian church was deeply troubled. Yet out of those troubles have come some of the most magnificent passages in the Bible as Paul brought to bear on them the great and changeless principles of the gospel.

The interaction of the divine and the human that underlies Paul's understanding of his ministry is as significant and important for us today as it was for him and his immediate readers. In the insights it affords, we can find help in understanding the interworking of grace and gumption in our own everyday lives.

—W. T. PURKISER

INTRODUCTION

One of the most fascinating studies in Scripture concerns the relationship between the divine and the human. Every aspect of our Christian faith is a unique blending of these two. There is God's side, first and foremost. But there is also our human side apart from which God does not operate. "Without God, we cannot. Without us, He will not."

We see this blending and interaction worked out in many ways. We see it in the Person and life of Christ Jesus, the God-man—at once totally divine and perfectly human. To neglect either the deity or the humanity of our Lord is to miss what makes Him what He is, the "one mediator between God and men, the man Christ Jesus" (1 Tim. 2:5).

We see it in the Bible, written by men who "spoke from God as they were carried along by the Holy Spirit" (2 Pet. 1:21). Herein is the power of the Book. It is the word of redemption written by redeemed men witnessing to what God has done. At the same time it is the Word of God, "perfect . . . trustworthy . . . right . . . radiant . . . pure . . . [and] sure" (Ps. 19:7-9).

We see it again in the Church—divine and human, universal and particular, perfect yet faulty, one and many, organism and organization, Body of Christ and brotherhood of believers.

Most vividly we find in ourselves both the power of God and the frailty of man. We are given grace, but we must respond in obedience and faith. We may have our hearts in tune with heaven, but we must live out our lives on earth. We march to the beat of another world, but we move in the midst of a multitude who do not hear the drums.

All of this is, of course, reasonably clear. Yet so often we miss the obvious. The divine and the human belong together. But people are forever getting them separated. It is not easy to hold the balance. They are so different as to seem contradictory, and we find ourselves caught up in a living paradox.

One can trace the growth of entire systems of doctrine to a simple failure to hold in balance these two essential sides to the Christian faith. Some put all their emphasis on the divine side. They stress the sovereignty of God. Taken to its extreme, such an emphasis leads to belief in unconditional predestination—the view that God has from all eternity decided the life course and eternal destiny of every individual in the universe.

Others put their emphasis on man's side. The result is a deistic sort of humanism in which the whole of human life is placed within the possibility and responsibility of our self-sovereignty—a cult of self-improvement that ends in frustration and futility.

Yet here as almost everywhere the truth is not in the shallow extremes on either side. The truth is in midstream. Only there is the channel clear enough and deep enough to carry the load.

I. IN EARTHEN VESSELS

It is with this general question that the apostle Paul deals in the fourth chapter of 2 Corinthians. "We have this treasure," he says, "in earthen vessels" (v. 7, KJV) or "jars of clay." The treasure is God's gift; the earthen vessels are our human selves.

In all honesty, we must note that the context is Paul's magnificent defense of his apostolic mission against the questions that had been raised in Corinth. But the principle he states applies to the broader issues with which we are here concerned.

How much is implied in the "treasure," we will examine in more detail shortly. Here let it be said that we must never minimize the riches God has given us in Christ our Lord. What the power of God does for us is in truth nothing short of a miracle.

"He anointed us, set his seal of ownership on us, and put his Spirit in our hearts as a deposit, guaranteeing what is to come," shouts the apostle (2 Cor. 1:21-22).

"Thanks be to God, who always leads us in triumphal procession in Christ and through us spreads everywhere the fragrance of the knowledge of him," he says (2:14).

"We, who with unveiled faces all reflect the Lord's glory, are being transformed into his likeness with ever-increasing glory, which comes from the Lord, who is the Spirit" (3:18).

"God, who said, 'Let light shine out of darkness,' made his light shine in our hearts to give us the light of the knowledge of the glory of God in the face of Christ" (4:6).

"Christ in you, the hope of glory" (Col. 1:27), is a treasure beyond man's power to calculate.

Yet right along with this runs another truth. We have this treasure in earthen vessels, jars of clay, "common earthenware" (Phillips), "a frail vessel of earth" (Moffatt). God works within the limits of our humanity. We are still fallible human beings, living in an imperfect world, and conditioned by a hundred factors over which we have no control—some of which can never be changed this side of the final resurrection. We will never in this life get beyond our need for "the compassion of God and the charity of men."[1]

I would not go so far as one young preacher who took these words as his text and named his sermon "The Glory of the Cracked Pot." But some of the vessels do get chipped. They are marred, and indeed sometimes cracked. The Psalmist long before had said, "As a father has compassion on his children, so the Lord has compassion on those who fear him; for he knows how we are formed, he remembers that we are dust" (103:13-14). What God remembers, we would better not forget.

II. THE NEED FOR UNDERSTANDING

It would seem that these things would not need to be said. Yet most of the opposition to holiness from without and most of the frustration and disappointment of holiness people within comes from failure to understand the simple fact that we are human and are subject to human frailty.

For most of us, the greatest tensions are within ourselves. We find less difficulty in worshiping a divine-human Lord, reading a divine-human Bible, and belonging to a divine-human Church than we do in coming to terms with the pressures of our own lives.

Yet the Bible never pictures us as anything other than what we are. In the beginning, God made man of the dust of the ground, then breathed into him the breath of life. We were created and we live at the intersection of two worlds. We feel both the pull of heaven and the drag of earth.

When we are converted and sanctified, we are freed from the corruption of sin in our humanity. But we are not transformed into little gods, or even made into angels. We are, as someone quipped, "God's but not gods"; we are "Christ's but not Christs." Converted and cleansed humanity is still humanity—or perhaps we could say, true humanity for the first time. To be a Christian is to experience the power and grace of God. But it is also to live among men and women who have not known that power and grace. And it is to wrestle with the residual effects of sin in our own bodies and personalities, living in hope of a final redemption (Rom. 8:23-24).

We can live effective Christian lives only as we know personally Christ's redeeming grace. All begins with the work of God within. But having experienced God's power, we live

12

it out in the framework of daily life with all its perplexities, anxieties, and hardships. There is no failure on God's side. The limitations, hesitancies, and shortcomings are all on our side.

Part of our difficulty lies in our fondness for simple, sweeping formulas that fit all situations. It is easier to think in terms of molds and patterns that are fixed and unchanging than it is to think in terms of the dynamic variety of life. We can handle bricks more easily and confidently than we can boys or girls. But God is dealing with people, not patterns; with men, not molds; with boys, not bricks. It is sin that makes stereotypes. The saints—when they are saints—are refreshingly different.

We sometimes tend to think, for example, that the experience of heart holiness is the solution to every problem, the automatic answer to every question, the sure cure for every defect of mind and soul. Then when it does not work out that way, the doctrine has been blamed rather than our defective understanding.

III. HOLINESS AND OUR HUMAN PROBLEMS

Holiness does indeed have a bearing on our human problems. But it does not automatically solve them all. Basically and essentially, it solves the greatest: the problem of inner sin—that "law of sin and death" that is "hostile to God" and "does not submit to God's law, nor can it do so," about which Paul writes in Rom. 8:2-7.

This in itself is a tremendous victory. But it isn't the end of the war. Sin within may be destroyed by the stroke of the heavenly Executioner's sword; but sin without is still very real, and the devil does not die when we are sanctified.

To borrow terms from the logic of science, perhaps we should say that the experience of entire sanctification is a *necessary* condition for the best solution to our human prob-

13

lems, but a *sufficient* condition only for the sin problem. A necessary condition is one that must be present for the desired result to occur. A sufficient condition is one that always and without fail produces the given result.

To illustrate: Gasoline in the tank is a necessary condition to run an automobile, but it is not a sufficient condition. One may have gas in the tank, and still not be able to run the car if the battery is dead. On the other hand, a hole in a tire is a sufficient condition for a flat. You don't need anything else. Whenever there is a hole in the tire, it goes flat—however good the valve or the tread may be.

It must be admitted that a necessary condition is indeed necessary. You can have all the gas your tank will hold and still be stalled if you have no spark. But you may have all the spark that high-powered plugs will deliver and still not move an inch if the tank is dry.

To claim that holiness is a necessary condition for spiritual victory means that if it is neglected or rejected, defeat is certain. No Christian can win his spiritual warfare if he must fight on two fronts—the enemy on the outside, and the fifth column of a carnal disposition on the inside. But we must face the fact that there are some human problems for which holiness is not the sole answer. The best of saints still have a long road to travel. There are rough places to be smoothed, kinks of mind and personality to be straightened out, infirmities to be faced, and weaknesses to be strengthened. Weakness is not necessarily wickedness. One may have the fullness of the Spirit and still need help with personal problems of emotional adjustment.

IV. A Creative Synthesis

The New Testament holds a creative tension between the assurance of spiritual victory and the possibility of human failure. We have not always been as successful. Yet it was a major contribution of John Wesley to Christian theology, as Melvin Dieter has pointed out, to develop "a creative synthesis in which elements of divine revelation and human experience, which are polarized in other theological systems, exists together in a viable tension."[2] Wesley developed a true synergism, that is, a doctrine of interaction between God and man. He never wavered in his conviction of the absolute sovereignty of the Lord God. But he recognized the necessity of human response in that measure of genuine freedom implied in the biblical demand for faith and obedience.

As difficult as it may be, we must preserve this synthesis, this balance between easier extremes. If we are to clarify our message for our generation, we must grapple with the practical difficulties that arise in relating the divine and the human. Theoretically, it would seem easy; practically, it is a demanding task. We must make it clear how much the Wesleyan message differs from the shallow triumphalism of our day that lacks both a vision of the Cross and a theology of suffering.[3]

V. DIFFICULTIES

We must also clear away our own false expectations. It is probably not possible to expect too much from the experience of fullness in the Holy Spirit; but it certainly is possible to expect too sweeping results. We may be hoping to see in full salvation (sanctification) only what can rightfully be anticipated in final salvation (glorification). We could be expecting in a moment of time what really comes only from a lifetime of growth. Then when the expected results do not occur, disillusionment, discouragement, and depression set in. More spiritual fatalities occur through discouragement and depression than through pride or deliberate disobedience.

We have had heroic models of the sanctified life. Many

of its advocates have been men and women of unusual dedication and outstanding gifts. One unexpected result is our tendency to feel that if we had what they had in the measure of the grace of God, we should be as outstanding as they. But this is not necessarily the case. Peter preached in Jerusalem on the first Christian Day of Pentecost and 3,000 were converted (Acts 2:14-41). Paul preached there on the same spot 30 years later and they almost killed him (Acts 22:1-25). The difference was not in the measure of grace possessed by the speakers. It was in the circumstances and condition of the hearers. You can throw a lighted torch into a tinder-dry forest and get a major fire. You can throw the same torch into a swamp and it smolders and dies.

There are difficult questions that face us in this general area. At this point, at least, faith is easier than the understanding it seeks. There are no easy, glib answers. For one thing, the Bible is not as explicit in some matters as we might wish. Its great principles are clear; we do not always quickly see their applications in a changing world.

There is always the danger of rationalization. Acts, practices, and attitudes that are essentially sinful may be passed off as unavoidable human weaknesses. One man's carnality can become another man's humanity.

In 1919, H. A. Baldwin wrote the classic *Holiness and the Human Element.* He noted two extremes in the holiness movement. One so completely set aside the human element "as to intimate that the life of a holy man will be all but angelic." The other "allows so much for the human that, in some respects, there will be very little difference between the life of the sanctified and that of the sinner."[4] Fifty-five years later, Leon and Mildred Chambers noted the same extremes: "Some would make the experience of sanctification mean too little. Others, however, would insist upon a perfection that would rob man of his humanity."[5]

Some of our difficulties in this area are semantic. That is, they arise from the understanding of terms. Such words as *sin, holiness, perfection, humanity, fault,* and *infirmity* are each subject to a dozen definitions. There are, indeed, genuine differences in doctrine. Yet many confusions are the result of differing definitions of the words we use to communicate and explain.

Theology, it has been said, is "faith seeking understanding."[6] It is that indeed. But the order of the terms is important. Faith is first. Understanding follows. John's great prologue in the fourth Gospel states the same insight: Christ is full of and came to bring "grace and truth" (John 1:14, 16). Grace and faith come first; but truth and understanding must follow.

So it is with some measure of trepidation we approach this subject. There is much fallow ground here, untouched by the plow of Christian candor. The liability to misunderstanding is great. There is the risk of opening the door to rationalization, giving good reasons for bad attitudes and acts. But the values outweigh the liabilities, and we must accept the challenge. If we can enlarge our own understanding, we may develop greater sympathy for those who are struggling over the first miles of the Christian journey and have greater appreciation for the genuine piety of those whose understanding differs from ours. We can then better avoid the defensiveness that comes so easily to us—a defensiveness due less to courageous commitment to truth than to secret uncertainty about the foundations on which we stand.

CHAPTER 1

THIS TREASURE

Before turning to these "earthen vessels," we need to look at "this treasure" (2 Cor. 4:7). Over and over in Scripture there is the repeated comparison of the godly life to wealth, treasure, or riches. Among the Proverbs of Solomon is a beautiful gem:

The blessing of the Lord brings wealth,
and he adds no trouble to it (Prov. 10:22).

I. WEALTH IN CHRIST

The New Testament picks up the theme. Jesus himself compared the kingdom of heaven to a great treasure found in a field and to a pearl of great price—either of which was worth selling out all that we have in order to obtain (Matt. 13:44-45). The soul in its eternity is worth more than the world in its entirety, said Jesus: "For what shall it profit a man, if he shall gain the whole world, and lose his own soul?" (Mark 8:36, KJV). Our Lord warned us that the treasures of earth are perishable and uncertain: "Store up for yourselves treasures in heaven," He said, "where moth and rust do not destroy, and where thieves do not break in and steal" (Matt. 6:20). And the "teacher of the law who has been instructed about the kingdom of heaven is like the owner of a house who brings out of his storeroom new treasures as well as old" (Matt. 13:52).

We see the paradox of spiritual wealth in the midst of earthly poverty. "The grace of our Lord Jesus Christ" was "that though he was rich, yet for your sakes he became poor, so that you through his poverty might become rich" (2 Cor. 8:9). Paul himself often lived in want yet the preaching of his gospel made many rich (2 Cor. 6:10). James tells us that God has "chosen those who are poor in the eyes of the world to be rich in faith and to inherit the kingdom he promised those who love him" (2:5). The Christians at Smyrna, living in affliction and poverty, were yet rich, Jesus said (Rev. 2:9). Even the lukewarm believers in Laodicea could become rich if they would but buy "gold refined in the fire" (Rev. 3:18). "Those who are rich in this present world," on the other hand, are "not to be arrogant nor to put their hope in wealth, which is so uncertain, but to put their hope in God, who richly provides us with everything for our enjoyment" (1 Tim. 6:17).

God, our Heavenly Father, is "rich in mercy" (Eph. 2:4) and makes known to us "the riches of his glory" (Rom. 9:23) and "the riches of [his] wisdom and knowledge" (Rom. 11:33). He lavishes upon us the riches of His grace (Eph. 1:7; 2:7) and reveals "the riches of his glorious inheritance" (Eph. 1:18).

But God's greatest gift is His incarnate, risen, and ascended Son. Paul sings of "the unsearchable riches of Christ" (Eph. 3:8) and "the riches of . . . Christ in you, the hope of glory" (Col. 1:27). In Christ "are hidden all the treasures of wisdom and knowledge" (Col. 2:3). The rule and guide of our lives is "the word of Christ" which dwells in us richly (Col. 3:16). God meets all our needs "according to his glorious riches in Christ Jesus" (Phil. 4:19) and "Godliness with contentment is great gain" (1 Tim. 6:6).

Happily, this richly endowed fellowship of faith is not an

exclusive society closed to all but a chosen few: "The same Lord is Lord of all and richly blesses all who call on him" (Rom. 10:12). Paul's great prayer for his friends in Christ was "that out of his glorious riches he may strengthen you with power through his Spirit in your inner being, so that Christ may dwell in your hearts through faith" (Eph. 3:16-17). No unredeemable harm can come to such: they can say with Paul, "To me, to live is Christ and to die is gain" (Phil. 1:21).

II. THE RICHES OF HIS GRACE

What are "the unsearchable riches" that are this treasure we have in earthen vessels? There are many ways it might be summarized, but a recurrent note throughout makes it clear that "Christ in you, the hope of glory" is the secret of it all. The measure of God's loving concern for us is reflected in Paul's words in Rom. 5:8, "God demonstrates his own love for us in this: While we were still sinners, Christ died for us."

"While we were still sinners," before we ever came to Him, He came to us in a dimension of grace theologians have come to call "prevenient." *Prevenient* simply means "That which comes before" and speaks of God's reaching out to sinful man. But the older form of the word is important: prevenient grace is preventing grace. It is grace operating in our lives to restrain the expression of hearts by nature "deceitful above all things and beyond cure" (Jer. 17:9), that is, apart from the power of God.

God's grace not only builds the hospital at the foot of the cliff to mend and restore those who have gone over the edge; it also builds a fence along the top of the cliff to help avert their falling. Such are the influence of godly homes, the preaching and teaching of the Word, and the restraining influence of conscience quickened by the light that lights every man who comes into the world (John 1:9).

Prevenient grace leads to pardoning grace, the riches of

20

forgiveness, and a new life. Our God is "rich in mercy." Though "all have sinned and fall short of the glory of God," yet we "are justified freely by his grace through the redemption that came by Christ Jesus" (Rom. 3:23-24). Justification, in John Wesley's terms, is "Christ *for* us." He offered himself as a Sacrifice in our place, that through His atoning death we might be reconciled to God.

But Christ for us is also Christ *in* us as a new life-principle, changing us inwardly in the miracle of a new birth. One of the tragedies of modern Christianity is the number of good people whose whole conception of the Christian life is perpetual forgiveness for perpetual sinning. But over and over, the Bible proclaims the regenerating grace of God that delivers us not only from the guilt of sin but from the all-but irresistible power of sin as well.

Stephen Neill is undoubtedly correct when he writes, "The achievement of Christian people will certainly not be higher than the ideal that is set before them." Then he asks,

> If this is the picture of the Christian's life ("committing daily the same old sins without end;" "we sin daily in words and deeds, by commission and omission"—Luther, *Larger Catechism*) that is being set forth, if the message concerns only a deliverance from the wrath of God, and not a Deliverer who can set us free here and now from the power and dominion of sin, why in the world should anyone ever come to church?[1]

III. GOD'S INDWELLING PRESENCE

But our treasure does not stop with the riches of pardon and the new life, as great in value as these are. It includes the riches of God's indwelling presence through His Spirit. This is what Paul meant when he prayed "that out of his glorious riches he may strengthen you with power through his Spirit in your inner being, so that Christ may dwell in your hearts through faith" (Eph. 3:16-17).

There is a note here that had been sounded by Jesus in the Last Supper Discourse with His disciples under the shadow of the Cross. He had used the reality of their love for Him as the basis for a challenge to obedience: "If you love me, you will obey what I command." Then He said, "And I will ask the Father, and he will give you another Counselor to be with you forever—the Spirit of truth. The world cannot accept him, because it neither sees him nor knows him. But you know him, for he lives with you and will be in you." But the promise does not end with the presence of the Comforter within, for Jesus added, "If anyone loves me, he will obey my teaching. My Father will love him, and *we* [Father and Son] will come to him and make our home with him" (John 14:15-17, 23, emphasis added).

It is a sad fact that many stop short of the full promise God has given. They are willing enough to receive Christ as Savior, but they draw back from His claim to be not only Savior but Lord. They may use the term *Lord* freely, but have no answer to Christ's question, "Why do you call me, 'Lord, Lord,' and do not do what I say?" (Luke 6:46). Not everyone who calls Him, "Lord, Lord," but "he who does the will of [His] Father who is in heaven" shall know the in-working power of His kingdom (Matt. 7:21).

Our human response to Christ as Savior is the confessing and forsaking of our sins in the attitude of repentance. Our human response to Christ as Lord is consecration—that total yielding of ourselves in service to "righteousness leading to holiness" for which Paul pled in Rom. 6:13, 19, and 12:1-2.

While our human response to the Lordship of Jesus is consecration, God's side is that infilling of the Holy Spirit in which His sanctifying Lordship cleanses the self of its inherited rebelliousness and fills it with the love of God. H. Orton Wiley wrote that the saving work of the Holy Spirit may be distinguished broadly under two main heads. He is "the Lord and Giver of life," and He is "a sanctifying Presence." The first, as Wiley notes, belongs to the realm of the birth of the Spirit; the second is the baptism or fullness of the Spirit, "a subsequent work by which the soul is made holy . . . known as entire sanctification."[2]

Holiness, then, is life under the Lordship of Christ in consecration; cleansed, sealed, and empowered by His Holy Spirit of promise.

Many who do not use the terms that holiness people prefer are coming to experience what those terms really represent. An interesting, if somewhat controversial, book by Richard Quebedeaux is titled *The Young Evangelicals.* Quebedeaux writes,

> The New Evangelicals are again emphasizing the necessity of meaningful sanctification following regeneration (or the new birth). For them, it is not enough merely to be pardoned of sin; one must also be *cleansed* from sin and adequately equipped thereby to live a new life. The life in Christ, moreover, is seen to be just as important as correct doctrine. And while legalism and moralism are censured unequivocally, there is a mounting interest among the New Evangelicals in the "social holiness" characteristics of John Wesley. In a word, Christian practice is to be understood as the *indispensible* consequence or fruit of a dynamic faith.[3]

Oswald Chambers was a prophetic voice in the holiness movement in the early years of this century. He said much that we have not as yet fully appreciated. There is real value in the caution he voices:

> Holiness is not an attainment at all, it is the gift of God, and the pietistic tendency is the introspection which makes me worship my own earnestness and not take the Lord seriously at all. It is a pious fraud that suits the natural man immensely. God makes holy, *He* sanctifies, *He* does it all. All I have to do is to come as a spiritual pauper, not ashamed to beg, and let go of my right to myself and act on Romans xii. 1-2. It is never "*Do, do,* and you'll be" with the Lord, but "*Be, be,* and I will *do* through you." It's a case of "hands up" and letting go, and then entire reliance on Him.[4]

That such reliance involves our active cooperation is certainly true. But it is important to recognize that

> *Every virtue we possess,*
> *And every victory won,*
> *And every thought of holiness*
> *Are His alone.*[5]

Such an attitude will save us from the temptation to spiritual pride and from becoming what Albert Outler described as "doctrinaire, simplistic and insufferably self-righteous."[6] Frances Ridley Havergal said it well:

> *Holiness by faith in Jesus,*
> *Not by effort of thine own,*
> *Sin's dominion crushed and broken*
> *By the power of grace alone.*
> *God's own holiness within thee,*
> *His own beauty on thy brow:*
> *This shall be thy pilgrim brightness,*
> *This thy blessed portion now.*[7]

IV. ENDURING VALUES

A fourth aspect of the unsearchable riches of Christ is assurance of His continued presence. Christ *for* us is our justification; Christ *in* us is our sanctification; Christ *with* us is our security. Neither the new birth nor entire sanctification would have much meaning simply as historical moments in our spiritual biographies. Their value is their enduring results. It is the ongoing presence of the Father and Son in the indwelling Spirit that not only saves and sanctifies but keeps us from the evil that is in the world.

All too often we have acted as if what God had done for us was an end for which we would strive, a goal to be reached, the destination of our earthly journey. Rather it is the beginning, the starting point, the commencement of our pilgrimage. An author unknown to me has put it in a series of succinct statements:

> *What we give He takes;*
> *What He takes He cleanses;*
> *What He cleanses He fills;*
> *What He fills He uses.*

A final essential aspect of the riches of God's grace is one that is particularly meaningful for us in the changing scenes of this earthy life. It is the prospect for the future. At the darkest moment of his missionary work in Burma, Adoniram Judson proclaimed the future "as bright as the promises of God."

The Christian faith indeed looks back to its foundations in history and experience. But it is incurably forward-looking. What we experience at the present time, whether of good or of ill, bane or blessing, is "not worth comparing with the glory that will be revealed in us" (Rom. 8:18). "Now we are the children of God, and what we will be has not yet been made known. But we know that when he appears, we shall be like him, for we shall see him as he is. Everyone who has this hope in him purifies himself, just as he is pure" (1 John 3:2-3). It will be worth it all when we see Jesus.[8]

We need to understand the earthliness of these vessels of clay—our human selves. To this effort we shall next turn our attention. But in our search for understanding, we must never forget the treasure God gives in these "unsearchable riches of Christ" (Eph. 3:8).

CHAPTER 2

EARTHEN VESSELS

The "earthen vessels" in which we have the treasures of divine grace represent an area in which theologians are taking new interest these days. This is, of course, the psychological century. Many have reacted against what is known as the psychology of religion because of its tendency to become psychology *as* religion. Psychology as religion will always be a broken bridge. But the legitimate concerns of psychology are of vital interest to Christians. For while Christian theology is the search for truth about God, it is always truth about God in His redemptive concern for weak and fallible human beings. No relationship can be understood in the absence of some awareness of the nature of both parties in the relationship.

Thoughtful Christians are "turning to the God who meets us where we are." It is not that the traditional theological themes of the Trinity, God the Father, the Son, and the Holy Spirit, are less important. It is that the "God-intended shape of human life" is becoming of more concern. It is being recognized that the correlative of Creator is "creature." The doctrine of God can lead us to better biblical understanding of that image in which we are created.[1]

A keen-minded layman posed some of the questions that underlie our study here:

> In describing sanctification, we use terms such as "entire sanctification," "sanctified wholly," "filled with the Spirit," and "a Spirit-controlled life." Yet we seem to turn right around and say that because we are human, because we are finite, because we "have this treasure in earthen vessels," we really cannot attain the kind of life these terms might indicate. Do the words we use apply only positionally in our relationship to God, whereas experientially we live on another level? Exactly how does the Holy Spirit affect our personal lives?[2]

That these are not easy questions to answer would be evident to anyone who tried. Simplistic answers are no answers at all. Our problems lie with both sides of the equation. In discussing the biblical terms that describe the treasure, we are apt to read into them meanings God never intended. And we are apt to misunderstand the nature of our human limitations. God does wonderful things in the redemptive grace of the Lord Jesus and in the fullness of His Spirit. But He does them in the context of a relationship with creatures who in the course of their earthly lives will always come short of His full glory.

I. Mistaken Expectations

No one has ever expected too much from the grace of God. He is "able to do immeasurably more than all we ask or imagine" (Eph. 3:20). His resources are unlimited. Our problem is not that we expect too much. It is that we expect the wrong results. "Expect a miracle" is good advice. The trouble is that many confuse miracles with magic. A miracle is God's personal intervention for the moral and spiritual good of His people and for the accomplishment of His ends. Magic is the vain attempt of the human will to control the supernatural for the accomplishment of human ends.

Many are disappointed because they expect instant solutions to all their problems. At the altar we find the answer to our fundamental relationship with God in regeneration and entire sanctification. It is not necessarily the answer to a whole complex of physical, psychological, and social problems.

What the grace of God does is to put us in touch with resources we would never otherwise have. But in large measure, the use we make of those resources is up to us. Over and over the Old Testament reports that "the Lord fought for" His people. But He did nothing for them until they picked up swords and shields and went out to battle.

Here is the true balance between release and responsibility. We release our lives to God but accept the responsibility for what He would have us do with those lives. Not to expect great things from God is to deny His power. To expect the wrong things is to invite disappointment, discouragement, and doubt. We dare not forget, as H. Orton Wiley aptly notes, that those who are "justified and sanctified still belong to a race under the doom of original sin, and will bear the consequences of this sin to the end of the age."[3]

A catalog of unrealistic expectations would be a book in itself. It is vain to expect immunity from trouble; freedom from temptation; sinless perfection; an experience that cannot be lost; deliverance from the ambiguities and contradictions of human life; freedom from blunders and mistakes; exemption from the necessity for growth and maturity; a perpetual emotional high; instantaneous sainthood; deliverance from natural instincts, drives, and needs; or an experience and life just like that of someone else.[4]

II. PARAMETERS OF HUMANITY

Our "earthen vessels" were created by God, corrupted by sin, and corrected by grace, but they are conditioned by our humanity. They are to be converted, consecrated, cleansed, and commissioned. But their final transformation awaits what could well be the next great event in human history: "Our citizenship is in heaven. And we eagerly await a Savior from there, the Lord Jesus Christ, who, by the power that enables him to bring everything under his control, will transform our lowly bodies so that they will be like his glorious body" (Phil. 3:20-21).

Paul's swift summary of the evidences of our humanness is given in 2 Cor. 4:8-9. "We are hard pressed on every side, but not crushed" reflects the pressures of the varying circumstances in which we live, the stresses that come to us from without.

We are "perplexed, but not in despair": we have intellectual problems; we don't have answers to all the questions. The term Paul uses that is translated "perplexed" is one of the New Testament words for doubt—not the doubt that is unbelief and disobedience, but the doubt that is seeking, reaching for answers, asking the difficult questions.

We are "persecuted, but not abandoned." In a narrow sense, persecution is opposition from others specifically because of a Christian commitment. In a broader sense, persecution is any opposition arising from the actions or attitudes of other people. Ninety percent of our problems are not from "things," circumstances, or conditions; they are from people.

We are "struck down, but not destroyed." Phillips translates this, "We may be knocked down but we are never knocked out!" These words hint at the physical problems that beset so many: illness, disease, accident, crippling and life-threatening occurrences or happenings that remind us so constantly of our vulnerability.

III. Created by God

Fact No. 1 in assessing our earthen vessels is the awareness that they are created by God. We are what we are not by chance, by the workings of blind law, or as the outcome of some sort of natural process people call evolution. The most elementary textbooks on physiology and psychology bear witness to a truth the Psalmist realized centuries ago: we are "fearfully and wonderfully made" (Ps. 139:14). To suppose that humanity could have evolved without purpose or plan is, as one recent writer said, like supposing that a Boeing 747 could come from a tornado in a junkyard.

For all the debate that has raged around them, the opening chapters of Genesis are crucial for the understanding of what or who we are. The climax of creation is described in Gen. 1:26-27, "Then God said, 'Let us make man in our image, in our likeness, and let them rule over the fish of the sea and the birds of the air, over the livestock, over all the earth, and over all the creatures that move along the ground.' So God created man in his own image, in the image of God he created him; male and female he created them."

A. The Divine Image

This is the concept of "the image of God," the *Imago Dei* of theological Latin. The biblical understanding of human nature starts here. Our worth as persons does not lie in our inherent goodness, as humanism would claim. It lies in the potential of God's creative purpose for us. Our humanity is deeply flawed, but we are of infinite worth because we are loved with an infinite love (John 3:16). A strange advertisement offered a reward of $200 for the return of a rag doll lost by a brokenhearted child. The doll was not worth two cents on its own. Its value was in the affection of the child who treasured it.

Precisely what the image of God in man is has been widely discussed. Many theologians distinguish between the "natural" image and the "moral" image. By natural image they mean those qualities without which a human being would not be human. But being in the image of God also includes the fact that we exist in a spiritual order rather than one limited alone to the biological. We have a capacity for self-direction or freedom of choice, an awareness of right and wrong, and moral consciousness. Also included are reason, intelligence, and a capacity for immorality.

Human beings alone of all earthly creations stand before God as persons—as subjects, not as objects. Man stands in an "I-Thou" relationship with God. We are persons to whom God communicates the knowledge of His will, and whom He deputizes to "rule over" the earth as His representatives. In a word, the natural image of God, and our capacity for His moral image, includes everything about us that distinguishes us from other forms of animal life. The human race is distinguished from other species as the immediate creation of God (Gen. 1:26).

The moral image of God, on the other hand, stands for righteousness and holiness, a right relationship with God, and freedom from sinful and rebellious tendencies or dispositions.

The natural image, then, is essential to humanness. If the natural image were significantly altered, the result would be a creature no longer truly human. In contrast, the moral image stands for a state or condition that may indeed be changed—as it was by sin in the Garden of Eden, and as it is by redemption through Christ.

In technical terms, the natural image constitutes *essentia,* the essence of our being; the moral image is the *accidentia,* qualities that may change without altering the essence. H. Orton Wiley used to distinguish these two kinds of qualities by reference to a red brick wall. The "brickness" of the wall is its *essentia.* You cannot have a brick wall without bricks. But the "redness" of the wall is its *accidentia.* A blue brick wall or a green brick wall is still a brick wall.

31

B. At the Intersection of Two Worlds

A further clue to our self-understanding is given in Gen. 2:7: "The Lord God formed man from the dust of the ground and breathed into his nostrils the breath of life, and man became a living being." Here is the first indication of the essential duality of our human state. We are spirit, created in the image and likeness of God who is Spirit (John 4:24). But we are also creatures of dust. Our physical bodies are akin to the earth. *Ha-adam,* the term translated "man" from Gen. 1:26—3:16 and from which the proper name "Adam" comes (Gen. 2:20; 3:17) is related to *adamah,* which means "soil, earth, country, ground."

While physically humanity is related to its earthly environment, the distinctive element in its creation is the in-breathing of "the breath of life." The result is, in Hebrew, a *nephesh chayyah:* a living being, or literally, a living soul. The term *nephesh,* "being" or "soul," denotes here, according to C. A. Simpson in the *Interpreter's Bible,* "A complete person."[5] The lexicon definition of *nephesh* includes a range of meanings such as soul, life, self, person, etc.[6]

We thus live at the intersection of two worlds. We are creatures of earth, living on a horizontal plane, sharing the environment with a host of animate creatures and inanimate objects. But we have in us the breath of life breathed into us by the Lord God and we are creatures of soul, self, personhood, the spiritual image of God himself. It is this vertical dimension that sets us forever apart from all other earthly creation and makes it possible for us to be not only creatures but sons and daughters of our Heavenly Father. This spiritual dimension is what makes it so completely impossible for the things of the world to satisfy our deepest needs. The Creator has left within us a "God-shaped vacuum" that He alone can fill. What, indeed, shall it profit a person to gain the whole world and lose his own soul? (cf. Matt. 16:26).

32

To *nephesh* (soul) in the Old Testament we must add what the New Testament says about the correlative Greek term *psyche*. There is, in fact, a remarkable coincidence in meaning between these two terms drawn from languages so diverse. "Soul," as W. E. Vine has noted, may mean the natural life of the body. But it also means the immaterial, invisible aspect of human nature, the seat of personality or the "self," the element in man that perceives, reflects, feels, desires, chooses, and purposes. It is, in the redeemed, "the inward man," the seat of the new life.[7]

C. Spirit and Heart

Closely associated with "soul" throughout the Bible are three other very significant terms. The first is spirit—*ruach* in the Old Testament and *pneuma* in the New. Without getting into the argument over dichotomy versus trichotomy (that is, whether human nature is basically two—body, and spirit/soul; or three—body, soul, and spirit), let it be said that the soul of the human being is described in Scripture as being of the nature of spirit, just as God in himself is said to be Spirit. There is at least a functional difference between soul and spirit. Soul is the self in its horizontal, its outward-looking, manward dimension. Spirit is the self in its vertical, its upward, Godward dimension. It is the fact that we are spirit/soul that makes it possible for us to relate to God.

Then, this living person is also characterized by what the Bible calls "heart" (Hebrew, *leb*; Greek, *kardia*). Heart is the all-inclusive term that stands for the whole inwardness of human life, defined by Arndt and Gingrich as "the whole inner life with its thinking, feeling, and volition."[8] It is, as Wilber Dayton has said, "the 'control room' of the soul, by which one functions as a self-conscious and self-determining being."[9]

It is of the heart that Scripture most often affirms moral quality. The heart is "deceitful above all things, and desperately corrupt; who can understand it?" (Jer. 17:9, RSV). It may be perverse (Ps. 101:4), wicked and stubborn (Jer. 3:17), haughty and proud (Ezek. 28:2), depraved (Gen. 6:5; 8:1), and may be hardened (Exod. 7:14; 8:15, *passim*). On the other hand, the heart may have integrity (Gen. 20:6), be wise (1 Kings 3:12), be pure (Ps. 51:10), and be "circumcised" by divine action (Deut. 30:6; Col. 2:11). Indeed, the heart is preeminently the sphere of God's action within us (Rom. 15:6, 8-9; 2:15). It is "the hidden man" (1 Pet. 3:4), the real person.

D. Mind

Along with heart is "mind." In our English translations of the Old Testament, mind is sometimes used to translate the terms usually rendered "soul" and "heart"—a witness to the overlapping meaning of all these words. In the New Testament, the Greek words translated "mind" mean the capacity for reflective consciousness, perception, understanding, feeling, judging, and purposing. The mind may be "doubtful" (Luke 12:29, KJV), carnal and fleshly (Rom. 8:7; Col. 2:18), vain (Eph. 4:17), or reprobate (Rom. 1:28). On the other hand, it may be humble (Acts 20:19; Phil. 2:3), responsible (Acts 17:11), spiritual (Rom. 8:6), fervent (2 Cor. 7:7), willing (2 Cor. 8:12), and sound (2 Tim. 1:7).

The mind is to be renewed (Rom. 12:2), conformed to the mind of Christ (1 Cor. 2:16; Phil. 2:5), recipient of the inwardly written law of the Lord (Heb. 8:10). We are to love the Lord our God not only with heart, soul, and strength as the Old Testament *Shema* had indicated (Deut. 6:5) but also with the mind (Matt. 22:37; Mark 12:30).

E. A Psychophysical Organism

To pull it all together, we may say that God has created us as psychophysical organisms, whole persons akin both to the dust from which we came and the God in whose image we are made. At the very core of our being is a spirit/soul with all the capacities of personhood: self-conscious awareness, self-direction, and the ability to think, feel, and choose. This is the inner self, the core of personal identity that comes into this world as an infant, grows through childhood and adolescence into maturity and on to old age and the transition to the eternal order—ever changing, yet ever the same; each one a unique, unrepeatable, irreplaceable, unexchangeable essence.

Yet this inner self is in dynamic interaction with an outer self, a body, through which it interacts with its earthly environment and other selves. The person is this total psychophysical being. There is no sharp contrast in Scripture between soul and body as there was, for example, in Plato, or as there is in much of our popular "folk theology." But there is a clear distinction. For example, we are not to fear "those who kill the body but cannot kill the soul. Rather," we are to fear "the One who can destroy both soul and body in hell" (Matt. 10:28). The human person is a conscious, thinking, feeling, choosing self (spirit, soul, heart, "inner" or "hidden" man) functioning in the closest possible way with and by means of a physical body. Something of the awe of it all was captured by the Psalmist when he wrote,

> When I consider your heavens,
>   the work of your fingers,
> the moon and the stars,
>   which you have set in place,
> what is man that you are mindful of him,
>   the son of man that you care for him?
> You made him a little lower than the heavenly beings
>   and crowned him with glory and honor (Ps. 8:3-5).

Yet the Bible never loses sight of the weakness and frailty of humankind. People are still

>   *like the new grass of the morning—*
>   *though in the morning it springs up new,*
>   *by evening it is dry and withered* (Ps. 90:5-6).

Balancing the dignity of man is his degradation; he is "akin to clod and cherubim." Always finite, and thereby distanced from the majestic perfection of the infinite God, the human race is no longer what it was created to be.

IV. CORRUPTED BY SIN

We do not have the full biblical perspective on our humanity until we move into Genesis 3. Here, in what has been called "the Fall," we find a record of the intrusion of sin and death into the human scene. In one dramatic scene of temptation and surrender to disobedience, the clue is given to what has become our human predicament.

In yielding to the suggestion of the serpent in direct disobedience to the command of the Creator, Adam and Eve set their own God-given sovereignty against the sovereign will of the Lord God. Although the word *sin* is not used here, the fact of sin is described and defined. Sin was no part of man's condition until this point. It comes as an intrusion. And it brings, as its consequence, alienation from God and the sentence of death.

Here is made clear the twofold nature of sin. Sin is disobedience, "a willful violation of a known law of God." But sin is also alienation from God, the loss of that fellowship symbolized by walking together in the Garden in the cool of the day. The moral image of God in righteousness and holiness was shattered, only to be regained in the redemption promised through the seed of the woman (Gen. 3:15). That the natural image of God, though defaced and corrupted, was not lost is seen in the necessary exclusion of Adam and Eve from the tree of life (Gen. 3:22) and in the sacredness of life for Adam's descendants by reason of that image (Gen. 9:6).

A. The Twofold Problem

Each of these points is important for an understanding of redemption. Sin as an act or deed in human life is not the result of ignorance or inability to do otherwise. It is rebellion against the will of God as we have come to know it. And what theologians call "original sin" is at root a racial alienation from God. Our depravity—an inescapable feature of human history—is the result of "deprivity" or deprivation. We are spiritually dead and morally corrupt because we are cut off from the life of the true Vine (John 15:1-6). The result is a malignant disease of man's moral nature. It is in Vincent Taylor's phrase a "self-coronation,"[10] an unnatural self-sovereignty, self at the center where God should be.

It is important to see that this change in human condition from the untested righteousness and holiness of creation to the corruption that throughout history has marred our existence is not a change in the essential nature of humanity. Sin is no part of human nature as such; it only distorts and ruins it. While sin is endemic in man, it is "part of his *condition, not* part of his nature."[11] Adam and Eve did not become more fully human when they rebelled. If anything, they became less than human; certainly, much less than humanity was meant to be.

Nor is sin a necessary result of our human limitations, our finiteness. Only God is infinite and only He is without limitations. But limitations are not sin unless they are self-imposed. Those we experience by reason of our humanity may indeed be difficult to bear and may keep us from reaching the heights to which we aspire. But they are not sinful unless the attitude that accompanies them is one of rebelliousness against God.

Nor are we to think of the sinfulness of our condition as

37

a "something" added to our essential humanity. We have fallen into the habit, partly under the influence of our Keswick brethren, of speaking of "the sin nature" as if it were an implant within our humanness or as if it in some way made sin an inherent part of the structure of the human self.

B. A Corrupt Condition

We would be wiser to follow the lead of the historic creeds of Christendom, which define "original sin, or depravity" as "that *corruption* of the nature of all the offspring of Adam by reason of which every one is very far gone from original righteousness or the pure state of our first parents at the time of their creation, is averse to God, is without spiritual life, and inclined to evil, and that continually."[12]

Original sin is not a thing, an entity, a "nature" coexisting with our humanness. It is a corruption, a condition that alters the life and consciousness of the self but which is not an essential part of its essence. As Wesley said, "From this infection of our nature (call it original sin, or what you please), spring many, if not all, actual sins."[13] It becomes, in Reinhold Niebuhr's terms, that "bias toward sin from which actual sin flows."[14]

The word *corruption* as descriptive of our sinful condition is a term used throughout Scripture. By sins committed, we have "corrupted [our] ways" (Gen. 6:12) and corrupt ourselves (Deut. 4:16, 25). In our sinful condition, we are corrupt (Ps. 14:1), and "a corrupt tree" cannot bear good fruit (Matt. 7:17, KJV—NIV paraphrases it "bad").

As Christians, we are "to put off [the] old self, which is being corrupted by its deceitful desires; to be made new in the attitude of [our] minds; and to put on the new self, created to be like God in true righteousness and holiness" (Eph. 4:22-24). It is through God's "very great and precious promises" that we come to "participate in the divine nature and escape the corruption in the world caused by evil desires" (2

Pet. 1:4). A notable parallel is Paul's great injunction: "Since we have these promises, dear friends, let us purify ourselves from everything that contaminates body and spirit, perfecting holiness out of reverence for God" (2 Cor. 7:1).

In our human experience, corruption is an irreversible process. But God brings life and health out of the corruption of sin, disease, and death.

V. CORRECTED BY GRACE

Our human selves are created by God, corrupted by sin, and may be corrected by grace. We have already noted the first promise of redemption to come through the seed of the woman in Gen. 3:15, the famed protevangelium. All through the Old Testament, God sought for an obedience to His law as the human response to the grace of His offered favor. The New Testament is the record of the incarnation of the eternal Son who by His life, teaching, and sacrificial death and resurrection made it possible for those born in the image of the first man, Adam, to be born again and to bear the image of the last man, Jesus. We who love God and are called according to His purpose are "predestined to be conformed to the likeness [literally, *eikonos,* image] of his Son" (Rom. 8:28-29).

This conformity begins in two great moments of grace we have already named as regeneration and entire sanctification, but it is a process that goes on all through the Christian life: "We, who with unveiled faces all reflect the Lord's glory, are being transformed into his likeness [again, lit., *eikona,* image] with ever-increasing glory, which comes from the Lord, who is the Spirit" (2 Cor. 3:18).

Christians living in the fullness of God's redemptive will "have taken off [their] old self with its practices and have put on the new self, which is being renewed in knowledge in the image of its Creator" (Col. 3:9-10). And in the context of the promise of resurrection, "Just as we have borne the likeness [image] of the earthly man, so shall we bear the likeness [image] of the man from heaven" (1 Cor. 15:49).

The (corrupted) image of Adam is in stark contrast to the image of Christ: "For as in Adam all die, so in Christ all will be made alive" (1 Cor. 15:22). Paul's great argument in Romans 5 for the triumph of grace over sin rests on the fact that "just as sin entered the world through one man, and death through sin, and in this way death came to all men, because all sinned . . . how much more did God's grace and the gift that came by the grace of the one man, Jesus Christ, overflow to the many!" (vv. 12, 15). As Adam was the head of a fallen and corrupt race, so Christ is the Head of a redeemed people. "Where sin increased, grace increased all the more, so that, just as sin reigned in death, so also grace might reign through righteousness to bring eternal life through Jesus Christ our Lord" (vv. 20-21).

The restoration by grace moves through two stages or moments. The first, as we have noted, is forgiveness and a new dimension of spiritual life never known before—justification and regeneration. This is reconciliation with the God from whom we were estranged both racially and by reason of our own sins. This is what Jesus described as a new birth, being born of the Spirit or born from above (John 3:3-7).

A. God's Total Demand

But the demand of the new life is total. "If anyone would come after me," Jesus said, "he must deny himself and take up his cross and follow me" (Matt. 16:24). Unless He becomes Lord of all, He will soon not be Lord at all. It is in the deeper surrender of the redeemed self, traditionally known as consecration, that life is brought under the Lordship of Jesus in the purity and power of His Spirit, and the corruption of our unsanctified natures is cleansed. This is what holiness essentially is.

It is important here to remember that this transforming relationship with God through Christ and His Spirit is related to our sinful rebelliousness, not to our human weakness. We are human creatures still, limited and fallible, committed to the will of God in an unfriendly world. Sanctifying grace relates essentially to sin; the discipline of our humanness is the work of the years. Paul gloried in freedom from the principle of sin and death through the indwelling Spirit (Rom. 8:2); but he held his body in subjection lest having preached to others he would himself lose the prize (1 Cor. 9:27).

B. Humanity and Carnality

Admittedly, the line between humanity and carnality is not an easy one to draw. It does not fall in the area of the feelings or emotions as has often been claimed. It is found in the realm of purposes, intentions, and motivation. It is not how you feel but where your commitments are that really marks the difference.

Our human selves are to be surrendered to God and sanctified, but they are not to be destroyed. We often use language that is confused and confusing at this point. We talk about self dying, being crucified and destroyed. This is poor theology. Self is the inner core of personal identity. It is God's creation. To destroy it would be to produce nonentities. What we mean is that the *selfishness* of the self is to be dealt with, its false self-sovereignty, its pretense to be the lord of life, its claim to the throne. But the self is not destroyed.

What we call carnality—the sinfulness of an unsanctified heart—is the corruption, the disease, the fever, the warp of our moral natures. The sanctifying grace of God cleanses the corruption, heals the disease, reduces the fever, and straightens the warp. But it does not destroy the essential self.

Paul put this all in one sparkling, if much-misunderstood, verse: "I have been crucified with Christ and I no longer live, but Christ lives in me. The life I live in the body, I live

41

by faith in the Son of God, who loved me and gave himself for me" (Gal. 2:20). There is a false "self" to be crucified, and an essential self to be controlled by the faith of Christ, in order that the potential self may be realized in Christ.

C. A Personal Encounter

This comes about by being brought into a new and dynamic relationship with "the Lord and Giver of life." We can never afford to lose sight of the personal dimension of the sanctified life. Whatever else it is, holiness is first of all the abiding presence of a divine Person.

Our language threatens our understanding of this truth. We speak of "the experience," "the blessing," "the work." Holiness involves all of these. It is a real and deep experience. It is, in Paul's finely turned phrase, "the full measure of the blessing of Christ" (Rom. 15:29), or as the KJV puts it, "the fulness of the blessing of the gospel of Christ." It is the work of God and of grace within our hearts, spilling over into our lives.

The trouble is, "experience," "blessing," and "work" are all neuter nouns. So we quickly fall into the habit of talking about "it." "Do you have it?" "Have you found it?" "Have you received it?" With questions such as these we probe ourselves and others.

Yet what we are most concerned with is not an "it" at all. The "it"—the experience, blessing, work—is an effect, a result. It is the Cause we much cherish—the Giver first, and then the gift. Here we deal not with an "it," a thing, a sort of spiritual rabbit's foot to seek, to find, to keep and perhaps sadly to lose. Here we are concerned with a Person.

The "experience, blessing, work, gift" is abstract. It is changeless, static. It tends to become a cold, mechanical fact. Quite the contrary, the Person who is our sanctification is all warmth, compassion, and understanding. He is with us through all the changing scenes of our earthly pilgrimage. He can give us the kind of help that can come only from a personal relationship with an all-wise and all-loving Person.

Without wishing to oversimplify, may we not find here one of the reasons for frequent failure among us? May it not be that many are living in the shadows—defeated, discouraged, lacking the radiance and loveliness of the beauty of Jesus, neither professing nor possessing victory in Christ—simply because they have never come to see that it is Christ Jesus himself "who has become . . . our righteousness, holiness and redemption" (1 Cor. 1:30)?

Such Christians have been seeking an "it," and an "it" can never do for them what the divine Person alone can do. They are cramped by legalism because they have never really known the love behind the law. They are chained to a static, mechanical, thinglike concept of the most dynamic and spiritual relationship in life.

This is the situation behind the cutting, sarcastic, and inexcusable remark of an unconverted man to his Christian wife, "I wouldn't have what you've got for a million dollars."

She told about it sadly and remarked, "He said *what*, not who!"

In his memorable essay on the 13th chapter of 1 Corinthians, Henry Drummond summarized the total change grace works within us:

> Souls are made sweet not by taking the acid fluids out, but by putting something in—a great Love, a new Spirit, the Spirit of Christ. Christ, the Spirit of Christ, interpenetrating ours, sweetens, purifies, transforms all. This only can eradicate what is wrong, work a chemical change, renovate and regenerate, and rehabilitate the inner man. Will-power does not change men. Time does not change men. Christ does. Therefore "Let that mind be in you which was also in Christ Jesus."[15]

Who we have, not just *what* we have, spells the difference between shadows and sunshine, defeat and victory. More than salvation, we need the Savior; more than sanctification, it is the Sanctifier; more than holiness, it is the Holy

Spirit. As A. B. Simpson long ago wrote,

> Once it was the blessing,
> Now it is the Lord;
> Once it was the feeling,
> Now it is His Word;
> Once His gifts I wanted,
> Now the Giver own;
> Once I sought for healing,
> Now himself alone.

VI. CONDITIONED BY HUMANITY

Our earthen vessels are created by God, corrupted by sin, and corrected by grace. But they are still conditioned by aspects of our humanity. As T. A. Hegre writes,

> Nothing is removed in the crisis of sanctification except sin, for God does not dehumanize us. The old nature is the human nature tainted by sin; the new nature is the human nature purged from sin—the very same nature in a different relationship. As we see it, sanctification is not the eradication of a nature at all but the cleansing of the whole personality of sin. No part of us can or should be removed.[16]

We have not always recognized the extent of the damage done by the Fall. We have understood the spiritual and moral consequences: alienation from God, and the corruption of branches cut off from the Vine. We have not always taken into account the physical, social, psychological, and emotional results of human sin. This is symbolized for us by the "curse" God placed in judgment on the serpent, upon Eve and Adam, and upon the environment. Its theological significance is summarized by the apostle Paul in Rom. 8:19-25:

> The creation waits in eager expectation for the sons of God to be revealed. For the creation was subjected to frustration, not by its own choice, but by the will of one who subjected it, in hope that the creation itself will be liberated from its bondage to decay and brought into the glorious freedom of the children of God.

44

We know that the whole creation has been groaning as in the pains of childbirth right up to the present time. Not only so, but we ourselves, who have the firstfruits of the Spirit, groan inwardly as we wait eagerly for our adoption as sons, the redemption of our bodies. For in this hope we are saved. But hope that is seen is no hope at all. Who hopes for what he already has? But if we hope for what we do not yet have, we wait for it patiently.

The facts of the case are that we are part of the frustrated, groaning, suffering creation. We suffer what have been called the "residual effects" of the Fall. Adam's sin—compounded by those of his descendants—has left humanity maimed, crippled, disoriented physically, emotionally, volitionally, and rationally. These effects go far beyond the moral and spiritual damage we have suffered.

The wider damage of human sin is most evident in the physical. By the very mechanisms of heredity, the sins of the parents are "visited upon" the children even beyond the third and fourth generations mentioned in the Old Testament (Exod. 20:5; Num. 14:18). Only a cruel and badly mistaken theology would attribute all human disease and suffering to the personal sins of the sufferers; but all human disease, suffering, and death is the ultimate result of racial rebellion.

Nor does the miracle of redemptive grace change all of this. We are to be saved from the spiritual and eternal consequences of Adam's sin here and now. But as we read in Romans 8, we are saved "in hope" (v. 24). We can never have bodies like Adam's body here. Our blessed hope is that "our lowly bodies" will be transformed "so that they will be like his [Christ's] glorious body" (Phil. 3:21).

"Now we are [the] children of God, and what we will be has not yet been made known. But we know that when he appears, we shall be like him, for we shall see him as he is" (1 John 3:2). As we have in this life "borne the [damaged] likeness of the earthly man, so shall we bear the likeness of the man from heaven" (1 Cor. 15:49).

CHAPTER 3

IMPERFECT PERFECTION

One of the classic terms for holiness has been Christian or evangelical perfection. It was the one John Wesley used most frequently, although he claims not altogether by his choice. It has been, and is, a term subject to great misunderstanding.

The typical attitude is illustrated in the story of the evangelist who had worked himself up to a high pitch. "We are all sinners and far from perfect," he shouted. "Do any of you know a perfect man?"

A meek, nervous little fellow stood up in the rear of the sanctuary and said, "I do, sir."

"What!" cried the astonished evangelist. "Do you mean to say that you know of a perfect man? And who was that, may I ask?"

"Yes, sir, I know all about him. He was my wife's first husband!"

I. A SOURCE OF CONFUSION

Evidence of possible confusion lies in such dictionary definitions of *perfect* as "In a state of complete excellence; without blemish or defect; faultless;"[1] "complete in all respects; flawless;"[2] and "lacking in no respect; complete; in a state of complete excellence; without blemish or defect; fault-less; of supreme moral excellence."[3] While all of these dictionaries include more modest definitions, those cited amply illustrate the kind of problems that arise when the terms *perfect* and *perfection* are used to describe Christian character and life.

We who have been "on the inside" are well aware that the absolute perfection described in the above definitions is not at all what Mr. Wesley had in mind, nor is it what is intended in the biblical references to perfection as pertaining to persons. As Albert C. Outler, one of the leading Wesley scholars of our present day, has said, Wesley found in his reading of the church fathers a view of perfection as a process rather than a state. This gave him a spiritual vision different from the static perfection of Roman spiritual theology and the equally static quietism of the "mystics." Wesley put together the ancient tradition of holiness as *disciplined* love with his own Anglican tradition of holiness as *aspiring* love to reach "what he regarded to the end as his most distinctive contribution."[4]

Wesley was fully conscious of the caricatures of his teaching drawn by his opponents. As he wrote in one of his letters, "I want you to be all love. This is the perfection I believe and teach. And this perfection is consistent with a thousand nervous disorders, which that high-strained perfection is not." What Wesley called "that high-strained perfection" was and is, indeed, the most dangerous perversion of a true biblical concept of perfect love. "To overdo is to undo," he continued. "To set perfection too high (so high as no man that we ever heard or read of attained) is the most effectual (because unsuspected) way of driving it out of the world."[5]

In truth, one of the surest signs of perfect love is a keen awareness of one's imperfections. One of the strongest incentives to growth in grace is the consciousness of faults and failures that maturity may overcome. As Augustine is quoted, "Part of this perfection consists in the recognition of our imperfection in truth and humility."[6]

II. Limits to Perfect Love

Even "perfect love" must be understood within limits. In one of his conferences, Wesley responded to a question: "But do we not 'in many things offend all,' yea, the best of us, even against this law (of love)?" as follows:

> In one sense we do not, while all our tempers, and thoughts and words, and works, spring from love. But in another we do, and shall do, more or less, as long as we remain in the body. For neither love nor the "unction of the Holy One" makes us infallible: Therefore, through unavoidable defect of understanding, we cannot but mistake in many things. And these mistakes will frequently occasion something wrong, both in our temper, and words, and actions. From mistaking his character, we may love a person less than he really deserves. And by the same mistake we are unavoidably led to speak or act, with regard to that person, in such a manner as is contrary to this law, and some or other of the preceding instances.[7]

Nor is the love that is perfected within us ever to be severed from its Source. "Our perfection is not that of a tree, which flourishes by the sap derived from its own root," Wesley wrote; "but like that of a branch, which, united to the vine, bears fruit, but severed from it is dried up and withered."[8]

Perfection in the sense in which most people seem to understand it today is impossible as a standard. Its value lies in its power as an ideal—pointing to the limitless possibilities of a God-filled life.[9] Nor is any lesser ideal worthy of one who aspires to be like Jesus. When a critic challenged Methodist Bishop Gerald Kennedy about his church's ordination pledge to "press on to perfection," the bishop rightly replied, "What would you want them to press on to?"

III. What Is Perfection?

Recent translations indicate that the biblical words traditionally rendered "perfect" have broader meanings. Among these meanings are terms like "complete, full, undefiled, sound, upright, with integrity." The typical New Testament word for perfection *(teleios)*—if we give attention to its roots—describes that which achieves its end or purpose.[10] There is certainly no claim that believers are to become perfect individuals or even perfect Christians. What perfection in its biblical sense stands for is the great good news that the grace of God brings believers into a right relationship to a perfect Christ. The perfection is His and His alone.

The late Francis Schaeffer became known as one of the most articulate interpreters of evangelical Christianity to college and university circles in our day. Schaeffer wrote a caution none of us should forget:

> It is not my victory, it is always Christ's victory; it is never my work or holiness, it is always Christ's work and Christ's holiness. When I begin to think and to grow in the idea of *my* victory, there is really no true victory. To the extent that I am thinking about *my* sanctification, there is no real sanctification. I must see it always as Jesus Christ's.
>
> Indeed, it is only as we consciously bring each victory to His feet, and keep it there as we think of it—and especially as we speak of it—that we can avoid the pride of that victory, which can be worse than the sin over which we claim to have had the victory. The greater the victory, the greater the need of placing it consciously (and as we speak of it, vocally) at His feet.[11]

A holy life is not necessarily a "perfect life"—untroubled and serene. It is the life committed to God's will as He gives us to know His will, lived in the power of His sanctifying grace.

IV. PERFECTIONISM

Actually, of course, the danger is that subtly and all but unconsciously "perfection" becomes "perfectionism." There is a valid use of "perfectionism" in relation to historical movements, but as an attitude of mind it is every bit as bad as it is said to be. Perfectionism places upon human beings strains they were never meant to bear. It often leads to depression, as we become aware of the gap between what we are and what we think we ought to be. It can result in low self-esteem, feelings of worthlessness—often masked by apparent conceit —and sometimes even in the face of outstanding success.[12]

Perfectionism is one of the most common roots of conflict between people. It leads to legalism and an unhappy, demanding personal life. It is in truth imperfection of the worst sort—the exact opposite of what perfection really means.

A perfectionist, for example, typically has great difficulty accepting forgiveness. He is usually one whose parents were very demanding, never satisfied with the child's efforts, and unforgiving of his failures. And by the same token, the person who cannot himself accept forgiveness cannot give it. People with legalistic and perfectionistic tendencies are not only hard on themselves, but rigid, demanding, and unforgiving with others.

Most of us cringe at the phrase "sinless perfection." When we are wise, we avoid it as carefully as Mr. Wesley said he did ("It is a phrase I never use"). We understand what it could mean if properly interpreted. We also know how easily it can be distorted and misrepresented. Better is the suggestion Andrew W. Blackwood somewhere makes that we speak of "sinless imperfection." Nor is sinless imperfection a contradiction in terms. The truth of the Scriptures is that God takes very fallible, faulty, and imperfect human beings, brings them into fellowship with himself, and cleanses them from all sin and unrighteousness by the blood of Jesus Christ, His Son (1 John 1:7-9).

V. UNDERSTANDING SIN

That any creature should be "sinless" is to many an absurdity on the face of it. The issue obviously hinges on what sin is and how grace may deal with it. To a wide segment of modern evangelicalism, sin is *any* deviation from an absolute standard of righteousness. Representative of this view, for example, is Charles Hodge, the noted Princeton theologian. "The law demands entire conformity to the nature and will of God," he writes. "If the law is so extensive in its demands as to pronounce all defect in duty, all coming short in purity, ardour, or constancy of holy affection, sinful, then there is an end to the presumption that any mere man since the fall has ever attained perfection."[13]

Bishop J. C. Ryle of the Anglican church draws the line even sharper by saying that a sin consists of "doing, saying, thinking, or imagining anything that is not in perfect conformity with the mind and law of God. . . . The slightest outward or inward departure from absolute mathematical parallelism with God's revealed will and character constitutes a sin, and at once makes us guilty in God's sight."[14]

It is perhaps fair to ask, Where is this law that pronounces all defect in duty, all coming short in ardour or constancy of holy affection, as sinful? Where is it written that "the slightest outward or inward departure from absolute mathematical parallelism with God's revealed will and character constitutes a sin, and at once makes one guilty in God's sight"?

It would not seem to be the law of Christ who said that the greatest of all the commandments is, "Love the Lord your God with all your heart and with all your soul and with all your mind and with all your strength . . . [and] your neighbor as yourself" (Mark 12:30-31). Nor would it seem to be the law known to the apostle Paul who said that "love is the fulfillment of the law" (Rom. 13:10). A more biblical understanding of God's requirement is given by Daniel Steele in a notable statement in the *Milestone Papers*:

> All that I am required to do is to love God with the full measure of my present powers, crippled and dwarfed by original and actual sin. When I do this I am perfect in love in the evangelical sense—not when I fulfill that ideal moral capacity which I should have if I had been the sinless offspring of a sinless ancestry.[15]

A. The Biblical Use of "Sin"

The propriety of using the term *sin* to include "anything that is not in perfect conformity with the mind and law of God [or] the slightest outward or inward departure from absolute mathematical parallelism with God's revealed will and character" (Ryle) I have discussed at some length elsewhere.[16] Let it suffice here to point out the disparity of such use with the clear statements of Scripture:

"Everyone who sins is a slave to sin. . . . If the Son sets you free, you will be free indeed" (John 8:34, 36).

"What shall we say, then? Shall we go on sinning so that grace may increase? By no means! We died to sin; how can we live in it any longer? . . . What then? Shall we sin because we are not under law but under grace? By no means! . . . Now that you have been set free from sin and have become slaves to God, the benefit you reap leads to holiness, and the result is eternal life" (Rom. 6:1-2, 15, 22).

"Come back to your senses as you ought, and stop sinning" (1 Cor. 15:34).

"He who does what is sinful is of the devil. . . . No one who is born of God will continue to sin, because God's seed remains in him; he cannot go on sinning, because he has been born of God" (1 John 3:8-9).

Archibald Hunter, though he comes from the same theological background as Hodge and Ryle, sets the nature of sin in clearer perspective when he writes,

> Sin is not a failure to live up to an ideal of human conduct which we have framed for ourselves, neither is it a crime—a transgression of the law of the state. Seen against the backdrop of eternity, it is rebellion against a holy God, so that, when we sin we are putting ourselves at a distance from God and creating a chasm between him and ourselves which we cannot, of our own efforts, bridge. Sin is radical alienation from the all-holy Father.[17]

We shall take a further look in a moment at some of the dangers in an excessively broad definition of sin. Here, we should drop a caution against too narrow a concept. To insist on full awareness of the moral quality of an act or upon its total willfulness is to move the limits in too far and to exclude much that would have to be called sin in any meaningful sense of the term. We may easily confuse ignorance with innocence. There is a willful ignorance for which we are fully responsible. Nor should we forget that habits tend to become automatic and unconscious without thereby losing their moral quality.

Too narrow a concept of sin lends itself to rationalization. We must recognize for what they are the unchristlike attitudes, prejudices, prayerlessness, preoccupation with the secular, indifference, and unconcern that characterize so many professed Christians. One may also concede that even faults and involuntary imperfections, as Wesley noted, require atonement and are in some sense therefore to be classified as sin "improperly so-called," but still so-called.

For these reasons, Hunter's term *rebellion* and its correlative term *rebelliousness* may serve to indicate what sin involves. Rebellion is action, or a series of actions, and defines the sins men commit. Rebelliousness is a condition that persists, the underlying motivation for the actions of the rebel. A rebel is still a rebel, even when he is asleep. Even a rebel in prison is a rebel until an inward change takes place.

B. A Practical Issue

But is this only a theologian's quarrel? Does it really matter much whether or not we class all imperfections as indeed sins? Is there not humility in the Westminster Confession of daily sinning in word, thought, and deed? Why not yield the point and call all our shortcomings and infirmities simply sins?

The basic biblical reason has already been suggested. Scriptural affirmations of freedom from sin do not imply faultlessness or perfection of conduct. "No one who is born of God will continue to sin" (1 John 3:9), but he is still liable to mistakes, faults, errors in judgment and conduct, and what Wesley called the thousand infirmities incident to our humanity.

Indeed, if all such deficiencies in attitude and action are classified as sins, then sin becomes in fact inevitable and unavoidable and there is no basis for excluding the truly culpable evils that result when moral principles are deliberately transgressed. On the contrary, our whole human moral consciousness distinguishes between the accidental and intentional, between what we cannot avoid and what we choose to do.

There is all the difference in the world between a forgotten promise and a broken promise, between a misstatement of fact made in sincerity and a lie. To the casual observer, the forgotten promise and the ignorant misstatement result in the same consequences as the broken promise and the lie. But the agent in each case knows the difference. Forgetfulness and ignorance are regrettable, and require confession and amendment when recognized. But they leave no residue of guilt nor do they result in broken fellowship with God.

There is all the difference in the world between an honest mistake or an unconscious failure to do the right thing at the right time, and the deliberate and knowing transgression of God's law, which the Bible describes as sin. The feeling-tone that accompanies human failure is *regret*. We should do better than we do. Mistakes must be confessed and forgiveness asked even for unintentional offenses. But the feeling-tone that accompanies sin is *guilt*. One who sins stands condemned at the bar of his own conscience and in the sight of God whose holy law he has broken.

VI. SCARS AND STAINS

Just as there is a world of difference between actions that are unavoidable and those that spring from choice, so there is a qualitative difference between the sinful condition of an unsanctified heart and what the psychologist would call "maladjustive impulses." Our human predicament involves not only sins committed and sin inherited but the scars we bear from preconversion and presanctification experiences. We experience impulses and propensities that result from the conditioning effects of experiences that go back into early life and even to infancy itself.

Admittedly, it is not always easy to tell the difference between scars and stains. The stains are caused by sin. They blacken and deface. They can be washed away only in the fountain opened at Calvary where Christ died for our sins. Scars, on the other hand, come from conditions or circumstances quite beyond our control. They result from wounds in the life of the human spirit, hurts that come from disappointment, betrayal, bereavement, sickness, mistreatment, and a hundred sources outside our control.[18]

For one thing, we must be very cautious about describing heart purity as freedom from inner conflict. Any conflict—as in temptation, for example—that impinges on

55

our consciousness is "inner." And in addition to the impulses toward sinful choices that arise in the corruption of a carnal heart, there are "the repressed complexes and maladjustive impulses which have been acquired in life experiences,"[19] which are not in themselves sinful at all.

A. Psychological Maladjustments

Emotional complexes and psychological maladjustments are not necessarily signs of inner sin. As Curry Mavis has noted, "Defense mechanisms and depravity are not the same."[20] These psychic scars are "accumulated and frustrated needs of the personality. . . . Acquired psychic reactions often provide urges to unchristian behavior [that may] give rise to a resistance to the will of God."[21]

Mavis indicates two spiritually destructive hazards that result from failure to distinguish such matters that differ:

> First, the believer may become spiritually disillusioned and give up all confidence in the phenomenon of spiritual cleansing. When he discovers that spiritual cleansing, for which he had believed, does not always remove the maladjustive impulses, as he has supposed, he may come to doubt the possibility of heart-cleansing. . . . Inasmuch as his inner sin and his maladjustments are confused, he neither prays for spiritual cleansing nor does he seek intelligently to resolve his maladjustments.
>
> The other hazard is even worse. Having trusted Christ for spiritual cleansing, the believer professes to be cleansed, but as time goes by, doubts and feelings of guilt arise. He then secretly fears that his heart has not been cleansed because of the presence of urges to wrongdoing that arise out of a dynamic core of maladjusted experiences. However, he continues to profess spiritual cleansing but it is in doubt and in insincerity. Nothing blights the spiritual life as much as an insincere profession of divine grace.[22]

When the sin problem has been resolved in forgiveness and entire sanctification, we are still creatures of flesh and blood and heirs to a multitude of defects and limitations that not only stem from our individual life experiences but that root back in the brokenness of our human state. Only three persons in all history have known the full image of God: Adam and Eve before the Fall, and Jesus of Nazareth. Apart from the Lord Christ, all the descendants of Adam's race bear the shattered image of God that is also Adam's image (Gen. 5:3).

B. Residual Effects of the Fall

The brokenness of our human estate is not only physical —the accumulated effects in our bodies of untold generations of men and women who have lived at least part of their lives in rebellion against the wholesome and life-building law of God. It is also psychological—the dimming of our mental, emotional, and volitional powers; and social— the disruptions of family and society that result from the selfishness and greed of unredeemed humanity.

These are the residual effects of the Fall. The very fabric of our humanity is disturbed, distorted, and damaged. We are but maimed and crippled, disoriented and disorganized copies of the original God planned. The triumph of His grace over sin is real and total. But William Cessna reminds us,

> Even a sanctified person has to live with his own life history, with any deprivations he might have had, with the traumatic experiences of his past which continue to remain dynamic within him. There is help for such conditions if one is willing to "work through" such involvements; but to say that these experiences are automatically "cleansed" at sanctification is to do injustice to the doctrine.[23]

And even though we may not be able to "work through" all our human problems here, we have the assurance that the moral likeness of Christ we have in measure here will be extended to full restoration when we are "like him, [when] we . . . see him as he is" (1 John 3:2). Until then, "we have this treasure in earthen vessels"—a fact we should never forget.

CHAPTER **4**

SOME PROBLEM AREAS

It is time now to look at some of the particular problems that arise in the life of holiness, given the earthen vessels through which that life is expressed in this world. There are many more than can be treated here. But some of the most pressing in terms of our modern life situation should be addressed.

The issues considered arise from a number of areas of human life: physical, emotional, volitional, and intellectual. However, no classification or particular ranking would seem to be significant. Such is the organic quality of life that any one affects all the others. Nor can each be given complete study here. Only aspects that most directly relate to the grace of heart purity will be treated.

I. ANXIETY

Many would consider anxiety to be endemic to the life of man. W. H. Auden spoke of ours as "the age of anxiety." Yet anxiety, worry, and the generalized fear of the unknown future have seemed to some to be unworthy of the best in Christian experience and a virtual denial of trust in the benevolence and power of God.

Part of our problem at this point is semantic. One man's worry is another man's sense of responsibility. One person's anxiety is another person's normal concern. There is a degree of anxiety that is a natural part of responsible living. It is like the tension of the strings of a violin—essential to the melody of life.

There is a difference also between a mild and "normal" anxiety and the more acute anxiety that imposes tomorrow's load on top of today's and quickly leads to depression. While some tension in the violin string is necessary, too much breaks it.

We must also remember that extreme pressure may push sanctified persons beyond the range of the emotionally healthy and into an area where they need specific healing. As Psychologist Malcolm Jeeves has said, "People with acute anxiety states or severe depressions are sick people and need help and healing."[1] And a fragile psyche may be more easily damaged than that of a person more sanguine in temperament.

The apostle Paul spoke of "the care of all the churches" (KJV): "Besides everything else, I face daily the pressure of my concern for all the churches" (2 Cor. 11:28). His burden for the young converts at Thessalonica was such that he said, "When I could stand it no longer, I sent [Timothy] to find out about your faith. I was afraid that in some way the tempter might have tempted you and our efforts might have been useless" (1 Thess. 3:5). In the area of the physical, as Leon and Mildred Chambers write, "Sanctified people experience threats to physical well-being and will respond with automatic responses. The nervous system is made in such as way that the emotion of anxiety is a natural response to threat."[2]

This is not to justify excessive worry or anxiety. But we need to understand it. Anticipatory anxiety tends to produce precisely the result feared. We are invited and should take advantage of the invitation more consistently than we do, to

59

"Cast all your anxiety on him because he cares for you" (1 Pet. 5:7). This is often easier said than done. But we may gain real help by heeding the advice of the songwriter: "Take your burden to the Lord and leave it there." And there is wisdom in the whimsical lines of the verses titled "Overheard in an Orchard":

> *Said the Robin to the Sparrow:*
> *"I should really like to know*
> *Why these anxious human beings*
> *Rush about and worry so."*
>
> *Said the Sparrow to the Robin:*
> *"Friend, I think that it must be*
> *That they have no heavenly Father*
> *Such as cares for you and me."*[3]

II. DISCOURAGEMENT AND DEPRESSION

Closely related to anxiety and worry are discouragement and depression. The psychological roots are much the same, and one may easily slip from anxiety into depression. It has been claimed that discouragement is inconsistent with holiness.[4] On the other hand, Olin Curtis remarked that "a saint in this world, in situations where Christ is not triumphant, can have a sort of discouragement which actually grows out of his supreme love for his Lord." While "there is very great peril in such a mood," the source of it is in human factors over which we may have little or no control.[5]

In fact, one with the highest aspirations in Christian service may be most tempted to discouragement by stubborn realities that fall far short of the ideal. The only way to avoid all tendency to discouragement is to have no expectations.

Depression also may have physical causes, quite unrelated to the quality of one's spiritual commitment. Hypoglycemia (low blood sugar) can result in an irritability and depression far from one's normal reaction. Menopause may result in severe bouts with discouragement and depression.

In Christian experience itself there is what has often been called "the dark night of the soul"—periods of aridity that come without apparent cause to some of God's choicest saints. Never one to lose an opportunity, Satan launches his most severe attacks in periods such as this. This is the trial of faith—"of greater worth than gold, which perishes even though refined by fire"—so that faith "may be proved genuine and may result in praise, glory and honor when Jesus Christ is revealed" (1 Pet. 1:7).

There are some important lessons at this point in the story of Elijah, "a man subject to like passions as we are" (KJV), "a man just like us" (James 5:17). After the tremendous victory on Mount Carmel, under the threats of Jezebel, Elijah fled to the wilderness, fell under a juniper tree, and wished to die. His emotional collapse was complete. Utter discouragement gripped his soul.

In this extremity, God did three things for Elijah. First, the Lord provided for the prophet's physical needs. An angel fed him and he slept soundly. Elijah's nerves had been stretched to the breaking point. His reserves were exhausted. Good emotional health is closely connected with good physical condition.

Second, God gave Elijah normal companionship. He directed him to find Elisha, and call the younger man to be his associate. The tendency of those discouraged is to withdraw from friends and Christian associations. This is the worst possible thing to do. One way to change undesirable moods is to seek the company of good friends. "We really do need each other."

The third step in Elijah's recovery was the challenge of a new task. Instead of sitting and brooding over his difficulties, the prophet was given a new assignment. To keep active, to find a job and do it wholeheartedly, is always a helpful cure for the "blues." There is wise counsel at this point from the pen of George Macdonald, the Scottish preacher, author, and theologian:

> Troubled soul, thou art not bound to feel but thou art bound to arise. God loves thee whether thou feelest or not. . . . Fold the arms of thy faith, and wait in the quietness until light goes up in thy darkness. Fold the arms of thy Faith, I say, but not of thy Action: bethink thee of something that thou oughtest to do, and go to do it, if it be but the sweeping of a room, or the preparing of a meal, or a visit to a friend. Heed not thy feelings: Do thy work.[6]

III. ANGER

A troublesome emotion to many falls under the general heading of anger. Some have suggested that being fully sanctified guarantees an unruffled serenity that is impervious to any sort of hostile reaction toward another. While holiness people have long exempted "righteous indignation" from negative emotions supposedly eliminated by the grace of God, the parameters of such indignation have been difficult to locate.

The Bible itself speaks of wrath and anger in two ways. The wrath of God and the anger of the Lord against evil are indicated over and over. Paul tells the Ephesians, "In your anger do not sin" (a possible quotation from Ps. 4:4), but he adds, "Do not let the sun go down while you are still angry, and do not give the devil a foothold" (Eph. 4:26-27). Jesus, confronted with the hypocrisy and stubbornness of the Pharisees, "looked around at them in anger" (Mark 3:5). One true measure of character is what it is that makes one angry.

Yet there is an anger generated by hate of which Jesus said, "Anyone who is angry with his brother will be subject to judgment" (Matt. 5:22). Five verses after his words, "In your anger do not sin," Paul says, "Get rid of all bitterness, rage and anger, brawling and slander, along with every form of malice" (Eph. 4:31). Since an overseer or pastor is "entrusted with God's work, he must be blameless—not overbearing, not quick-tempered, not given to drunkenness, not violent, not pursuing dishonest gain" (Titus 1:7).

We obviously need to be careful not to rationalize a carnal, ego-defensive anger as righteous indignation. It is not easy to tell the difference. In fact, John Wesley wrote the leader of one of his bands that "there is an anger which is not sinful, a disgust at sin which is often attended with much commotion of the animal spirits." However, he said, "I doubt whether we can well distinguish this from sinful anger but by the light of heaven."[7]

Anger is often an expression of a basic insecurity and fear. Perhaps in few other areas of experience are individual differences more evident than here. People differ widely in emotional makeup, disposition, and temperament. Some have inherited nervous systems that react faster and with greater intensity than others. Even the newly born show great variation in emotional responses to the same stimuli— from violent reaction, to mild, or slight.

Early environment makes a great difference. Children learn to respond in ways they find rewarding. The child who gets his way through a "temper tantrum" is likely to continue that sort of response in slightly more adult ways. "Antagonistic parents foster angry children."[8] H. Orton Wiley used to tell the story of an angry man whose minister told him, "You need to control your temper better."

The man's retort was, "Sir, I want you to know that I control more temper every day than you do in a year."

Nor does it quite answer the question to suggest that one has a right to be angry if he sees injustice done to someone else, but not if he is the object of the injustice. As William Cessna notes, "Injustice should evoke the emotion of anger whether the injustice is against us or someone else."[9]

Akin to anger is nervous irritability. We have already

noted the fact that changes in blood chemistry may result in irritability. Nerves are actually physical connectors that are subject to infection, disease, irritation, and malfunction just like any of the organs of the body. Fatigue, illness, stress, or pressure all influence the functioning of the nervous system and through the nervous system they alter conscious emotional states. A sick or excessively weary person is not to that extent normal. He may react in ways that are quite different from his normal reactions.

Here again individual differences are great. Some persons are high-strung and instantly reactive. Others are more placid. Some are hypersensitive to annoyances in the environment; others are more impervious to the same stimuli. Some are impatient and quick to react to hindrances; others are by disposition more accepting and less easily disturbed.

There is a significant passage in the diary of the saintly George Muller of Bristol. It is dated January 7, 1838, some eight years after Mr. Muller had entered the deeper Christian experience he called "the full surrender of the heart" and launched out in his magnificent work of faith. The entry notes:

> This is the ninth day that I have been kept from ministering in the Word. My head is in a distressing state, and, as far as I can judge, as bad as ever. It seems to me more and more clear that the nerves are affected. My affliction is connected with a great tendency to irritability of temper; yea, with some satanic feeling, foreign to me even naturally. O Lord, mercifully keep thy servant from openly dishonouring thy name! Rather take me home soon to thyself![10]

These words highlight a most difficult area. "Irritability of temper" may be the result of spiritual need—an unsanctified heart, a disobedient life, walking behind light. Yet even the most saintly may experience the "tendency to irritability of temper" and the satanic darkness of which Muller speaks. And we must avoid the twin perils of excusing the carnal and condemning the overwrought human. We want no compromise with selfish, explosive temper. Neither do we wish to join the "accuser of the brethren" and point the finger of condemnation at one whose heart may really be pure.

Even more difficult is the case when one finds such a condition in himself. It is very easy to yield to self-condemnation and surrender faith and trust in the cleansing Blood. Yet in the quietness of one's own conscience, open before the Lord, there is a clue offered in Mr. Muller's words. The feelings that puzzled him, he said, were "foreign to [him] even naturally." This was not the fruit of his own nature, either apart from or under the grace of God. This was an intrusion from without. The devil, said Thomas Cook, is adept at smearing mud on the Christian's windows and then accusing him of being a poor housekeeper. But the mud is the adversary's mud and has been brought from without.

IV. Feelings and Faith

We have considered some of the so-called negative emotions. What about the absence of high emotions of joy, pleasure, satisfaction, happiness, and tranquillity? The fluctuation of emotions such as these has been a trial to many sincere Christians. The joy of the Lord is indeed our strength. Does this mean that when joy subsides (or is incorrectly identified), God's grace is lost? This is a subject worth a volume in itself.

Many Christians enter the sanctified life expecting to find an experience of constant joy and blessing. Something of this is suggested in the very term we often use to describe the fullness of the Spirit—"the second blessing," or just "the blessing." Years ago a gospel song was current, the chorus of which expressed the thought, "My indigo factory burned down": ergo, no more "blues." The general idea of the song was that, since entire sanctification, all had been sweetness and light, an unbroken holy hilarity, a constant "mountaintop" or emotional high. That such is not the case scarcely needs proof. While there is blessing in "the blessing," it goes much deeper than the feelings. It is, as C. W. Ruth used to say, more a "killing" than a blessing!

Peace with God and the witness of the Spirit to a clean heart do often find expression in high emotional tides. It is then easy to make such feelings an indicator of spiritual condition. But as George Buttrick somewhere wrote, "A sailor measures his progress by the stars, not the thermometer in his cabin." One who goes around constantly taking his spiritual temperature is in a fair way to becoming a religious hypochondriac—that is, the victim of imaginary ailments.

The problem is, of course, that emotions have a way of changing from day to day. They are affected by factors in human life that have no relationship whatsoever to the spiritual and moral state. There is grave danger in identifying feelings with the grace of God.

Jesus is described as a "man of sorrows, and acquainted with grief" (Isa. 53:3, KJV) or "familiar with suffering" (NIV), whose tears flowed when He was confronted with the sorrow of His friends and the hardness of those He had come to help (John 11:35; Luke 19:41). Paul confessed his continual heaviness and sorrow of heart for his own nation (Rom. 9:1-2), and found occasion to need encouragement from Christian friends (Acts 28:15).

John Wesley wrote: "A will steadily and uniformly devoted to God is essential to a state of sanctification; but not a uniformity of joy, or peace, or happy communion with God. These may rise and fall in various degrees; nay, and may be affected either by the body or by diabolical agency, in a manner which all our wisdom can neither understand nor prevent."[11]

Emotion and blessing have an important place in the Christian life. A religious experience that had no effect on the feelings would not meet the needs of the whole person. It would not go far enough. But the purpose of emotion in religion is akin to the purpose of emotion in all of life. It is not primarily to be enjoyed, but to be employed. It is the natural prelude to action.

A. Emotion and Action

There is more in common between "emotion" and "motion" than the identity of six of the letters. God has given us feelings in the physical realm, for instance, as part of the preparation for some form of physical action. Fear is a good example. In fright, the glands pump additional adrenalin into the bloodstream, the heartbeat quickens, and the body is prepared for "fight or flight." Further, the appropriate action strengthens the emotion that inspires it.

The application to the spiritual life is not hard to see. God gives high tides of blessing and joy, not for the sake only of making us happy, but to prepare us for service to the Kingdom and to our fellowmen. Just as emotion in the physical life can actually be harmful unless followed by appropriate action, so blessing and spiritual joy miss their purpose unless they work out in heightened devotion. Emotion that is not expressed in devotion eventually dries up. Is this the reason some good people are not as blessed as they used to be?

But the very best state of grace will not guarantee high emotions all the time. Holiness is not synonymous with hilarity. Feelings are a by-product of religion, and neither its cause nor its measure. Rev. C. W. Ruth used to say, "Feelings are the most undependable dependence anyone every depended on"; and would remind us that the only man in the Bible who went by "feeling" was Isaac who as a result blessed the wrong boy!

Faith is the supreme condition for salvation. Conversion and holiness are relationships based, not on feeling, but on faith. We are saved by the grace of God through faith (Eph. 2:8). We are sanctified by the Holy Spirit through faith (Acts

26:18). We are kept by the power of God through faith (1 Pet. 1:5). Faith anchors to facts: the fact of God's promises, and the fact of our own consecration and obedience. Feelings are swayed by circumstances and may have no direct relationship whatsoever to the facts.

As we have seen, feelings are also conditioned by our physical state. The condition of a person's physical health and of his nerves makes a great deal of difference in the emotional responses in a given situation. Because of the variation in feelings, will and purpose must govern our lives and not feelings and impulses. Every Christian must learn to do what is right whether he feels like it or not. Conviction, not convenience, must guide our conduct. It is fine to go to church, to serve in the Kingdom, to read the Bible, and to pray when we feel like it. It is more important to do those things whether we feel like it or not.

While we cannot always account for the fluctuations of our moods and the changing tide of emotions, we need not surrender to them. The peril of uncontrolled moods is discouragement, the most potent tool the devil ever devised to defeat the people of God.

B. Obedience and Faith

There are two things more fundamental than feelings in the Christian life. These are obedience and faith. We must learn to "trust and obey," for there's really no other way to live effectively as Christians. When feelings of well-being subside, and "heaviness through manifold temptations" comes, then we should check our consecration and obedience. It is time to dig in and hold on by faith. Like all trials, "this, too, will pass," and our faith, so much more precious than gold, though it be tried in the fire, will "result in praise, glory and honor when Jesus Christ is revealed" (1 Pet. 1:7; cf. v. 6, KJV).

Since faith is a human response to the divine promise, it may also vary in strength and clarity. H. Orton Wiley used to say that when he could not enjoy the faith of assurance, he held on with the faith of adherence. Faith is an act of the will far more than the expression of an emotion. Faith reflects the basic purposes of our lives. It is a commitment in confidence to the reliability of a Person who is eminently trustworthy. And because faith links us to a power not our own, it gains a strength that is not its own.

The very human but thoroughly sanctified apostle Paul was tempted to discouragement and spoke of being weak, pressed beyond measure, troubled, and perplexed. Yet he never turned back and he never wavered in his purpose to serve the Lord in the obedience of a conscience void of offense toward God and man.

More important than fluctuating feelings are the posture of one's faith and the prevailing purpose of his life. It's not how you feel but where your commitments are. This is profoundly stated in Martin Luther's oft-quoted but ever relevant lines:

> *Feelings come and feelings go,*
> *And feelings are deceiving.*
> *My warrant is the Word of God;*
> *Naught else is worth believing.*
>
> *Though all my heart should feel condemned*
> *For want of some sweet token,*
> *There is One greater than my heart*
> *Whose Word cannot be broken.*
>
> *I'll trust in God's unchanging Word*
> *Till soul and body sever;*
> *For though all things shall pass away,*
> *His Word shall stand forever!*

V. DOUBT

Closely related to the battles of faith that arise through alternating moods is the question of intruding doubt. Doubts tend to press in under the same sort of circumstances that lead to low moods: our human vulnerability to disease, oppressive circumstances, and the shattering tragedies that come into the lives of so many good people. Doubt arises in disaster. It is not too hard to believe God when all goes well. But when betrayal, bereavement, or staggering loss comes, depression often follows and doubts push in.

Not that credulity is necessarily a virtue. Paul talks about those who believe a lie and are condemned in that belief (2 Thess. 2:11-12). "Easy believism" can lead to superstition and all kinds of error. It is not merely believing for faith's sake but *what* is believed that is important. God does not ask blind faith—faith with no basis, no foundation. What He does ask is trust beyond the evidence immediately available. Faith is always founded in fact; yet it always pushes beyond the facts directly at hand. Faith involves a "leap," an element of venture or commitment. This, in fact, is what makes faith commendable. There is no credit for accepting what is proved beyond possibility of doubt.

A. Kinds of Doubt

It is this factor of venture and commitment that opens faith to the challenges life presents. There are three different New Testament terms translated "doubt" in our English versions. One is a term that literally means "without a way," and stands for simple uncertainty, questioning, seeking, and exploring. Such "doubt" is the essential trigger to learning— reaching out for answers. There is no problem here: a thousand questions need never add up to a single sinful doubt.

A second term implies a struggle to grasp, a reaching out beyond the evidence, the stretch of faith to move beyond its present limits. It is the sort expressed by the man who sought Jesus for healing for his son and exclaimed, "I do believe; help me overcome my unbelief!" (Mark 9:24). "Stretch my faith beyond its present limits; help me grasp all that is available to me" is a prayer we may pray every day.

A third term points to doubt of a sort we need never have. It is a word that may be translated either unbelief or disobedience. It stands for doubt with a moral root, a loosening of spiritual moorings, a dying devotion, disobedience to duty.

There are some so-called intellectual problems that are really spiritual problems. Someone has remarked that for many folks what seems to be trouble with the Apostle's Creed is really trouble with the Ten Commandments. German philosopher Friedrich Nietzsche, the spiritual father of Naziism, said, "God is dead; all is permitted." The trouble with Nietzsche was, he had the wrong corpse. What he presented as his premise, "God is dead," was really a conclusion drawn from the desire that everything be permitted. One must get rid of God before he can affirm that just anything goes.

The remedy for this third kind of doubt is quick and easy, and there is only one solution. It is repentance, confession, and renewed obedience to God. The back side of genuine faith in Scripture is always obedience. Paul writes in Rom. 1:5 of the obedience that comes from faith, or as A. M. Hunter paraphrases, "the obedience which faith is." It makes no difference whether one talks about believing the gospel (Mark 1:15) or obeying the gospel (Rom. 10:16), they essentially mean the same. And James adds that "faith without deeds is useless" (2:20).

B. Dealing with Doubt

What do we do to keep a struggling, challenged faith from becoming victim to the kind of doubt that leads to defeat? We must first recognize that not all of our intellectual problems will be solved in this life. There are some things that we cannot settle until we know as we are known (1 Cor.

71

13:12). If getting to heaven depended on having all the answers, not many of us would make it. For a great many questions, there are no neat, complete, and final answers.

God simply does not choose to answer all our queries. No one had more question marks than Job, and yet no one had a better right to demand answers than he did. But he never did get specific answers to his agonizing "Whys." He never did find out what had been going on in his life. But what he did get was enough for Job—and it must be enough for us. He was given a revelation of God as One supremely trustworthy. As Frances Ridley Havergal wrote,

> We may trust Him fully all for us to do;
> Those who trust Him wholly find Him wholly true.

Furthermore, when faith is challenged by doubts or questions, we need to consider the alternative.

All doubt that is not sheer confusion is actually a negative faith. It is belief in the opposite. To doubt the existence of God is to believe that there is no God and that all that is has come about as the result of chance or blind law—which Dr. Edwin Conklin compared with expecting an unabridged dictionary from an explosion in a print shop. To doubt the Virgin Birth of Jesus—in the face of the clear declarations of the Gospels that Joseph was not our Lord's actual father—is to accept the idea that God introduced His Son into the world as an illegitimate child in total defiance of His own law.

This is the wisdom of the African proverb: "If a man does away with his traditional way of living and throws away his good customs, he had better first make certain that he has something of value to replace them."

C. Faith and Experience

Finally, we must always drive our Christian faith back to its basis in experience. Faith issues in life and is validated in experience. Faith may not have what, in a strict sense, could be called proofs, but it does have consequences that confirm it. This is the logic in the response of the blind man to whom Jesus gave sight. Challenged by the learned doctors of the law about the status of the One who had healed him, and faced with the claim that the Savior was but a sinner like other men, the questioned man simply said, "Whether he is a sinner or not, I don't know. One thing I do know. I was blind but now I see!" (John 9:25). Nothing could contradict the fact that he who had been blind could now see.

When Philip found the Savior, he went to Nathanael and said, "We have found the one Moses wrote about in the Law, and about whom the prophets also wrote—Jesus of Nazareth, the son of Joseph."

Nathanael was ready to argue. "Nazareth!" he said. "Can anything good come from there?" The truth of the matter was that nothing significant had come from there up to that time.

Philip's answer was the quiet invitation, "Come and see." Nothing can take the place of that. If you come, you will see; if you do not come, you will not see. It is just that simple (cf. John 1:43-50).

There is an eloquent paragraph at this point written by Norman Snaith, the distinguished British Old Testament scholar:

> This is the type of certainty which I, for one, have about God. It is not contrary to reason, and given its own premises, it is as logical as the rest. But it has its own premises, and they are premises which have their basis in personal experience of a Person. Nobody ever argued me into it, and I am quite certain that nobody can ever argue me out of it. It never depended on that type of argument. If anyone should ask me how it is that I am sure of God, I could give no answer except that it is the same kind of way in which I am sure of my wife. Just how it is that I am sure of that I do not know. It has been strengthened by the intimacies and mutual trust of the years, but it began. . . . The Christian is prepared to give reasons for the faith that is in him, but his faith does not depend upon such reasons.[12]

There is a "good fight of the faith" which we are to wage. By it we "take hold of the eternal life to which [we] were called" (1 Tim. 6:12). It is a fight made necessary by our human condition. It is by "the shield of faith" that we "can extinguish all the flaming arrows of the evil one" (Eph. 6:16). As we keep the faith, we are assured of "the crown of righteousness," which the Lord will give us on the day of His appearing (2 Tim. 4:7-8).

CHAPTER 5

TEMPTATION AND SIN

One of the most pervasive misconceptions of holiness, particularly on the part of those "outside," is to suppose that purity of heart, if such were possible, would place a person beyond the possibility of temptation. One scholar claimed that if there were no inward sin, temptation would have nothing to fasten on to and therefore would be impossible; that liability to temptation proves the presence of inner sin. Another study of sanctification mistakenly affirms that the Wesleyan position is that "the desire and possibility of sinning are extinct." Lewis Sperry Chafer, the Calvanistic theologian long associated with Dallas Theological Seminary, charged holiness people with claiming that "Because my carnal nature is destroyed, I cannot sin."

On the face of it, such views are refuted by the fact that Adam and Eve, in whom was no inner sin before the Fall, were subject to temptation and yielded. More conclusive is the fact that Jesus—holy, harmless, and undefiled—was "tempted in every way, just as we are—yet was without sin" (Heb. 4:15). Temptation is not our lot because we are sinful; it is our lot because we are human and living in an evil world where the most innocent desires may be corrupted and become an occasion for disobedience to God.

I. Temptation and Desire

The argument that temptation is impossible apart from the presence of inner sin reveals an inexplicable misunderstanding of the nature of temptation. The anatomy of temptation is clearly described in James 1:14-15: "Each person is tempted when he is lured and enticed by his own desire. Then desire when it has conceived gives birth to sin; and sin when it is full-grown brings forth death" (RSV).[1]

A. Sources of Desire

Temptation always starts with a desire seen to be at odds with one's master motivations, or his awareness of right and wrong. Some desires, indeed, arise from a sinful heart—a moral condition alienated from God and inclining the will toward rebellion against Him. Paul spoke of this in Rom. 7:8, "Sin . . . produced in me every kind of covetous desire." From such a condition, Paul goes on to declare, the law of the Spirit of life had set him free (Rom. 8:2).

But there are other desires that arise as we become conscious of unmet human needs and interests. The needs themselves are morally neutral. All human beings need security, food, clothing and shelter, satisfaction or sublimation of the sex drive, self-esteem, the love and respect of one's fellows, work that is significant, and what has been called self-transcendence—finding meaning in what is greater than ourselves.[2]

Whether these needs fall in the area of the physical, psychological, social, or spiritual, they are part of our native human equipment without which we could not function in a world like ours. The desires to which these needs give rise may be disoriented and disordered, and raised to an inordinate degree of strength. But they are part of the human constitution as it has been from Adam on. Wiley puts it well:

> While we remain in this life, however deep our devotion, or fervent our religious life, there are sources of danger within

us. In our nature, and as essential elements of it, there are appetites, affections and passions, without which we should be unfitted for this present state of existence. These are innocent in themselves, but must ever be kept under control by reason, conscience and divine grace.[3]

And there is hope of healing for sin-generated obsessions and compulsions that threaten to persist in the Christian life (cf. 1 Cor. 6:9-11).

The temptations of Jesus show how it is possible that desires that are in themselves entirely proper and right may yet lead to sin. It is not sinful to be hungry after going without food for an extended period of time. It would be sinful to satisfy that hunger by using the power of a divine mission to change stones into bread as in the case of Jesus—or in our case by stealing food. It was not sinful for Jesus to desire the allegiance of the nations. For this cause He had come into the world. It would have been sin to gain that goal by worshiping Satan rather than by enduring the Cross—just as it may be sin for us to achieve the right ends by the wrong means.

Desire in itself is obviously not sin. It is when desire has "conceived"—that is, when it has been taken in and cherished and impregnated by the consent of the will—that it gives birth to sin. It is not the *possibility* of sin but its *necessity* that is dealt with in the regenerating and sanctifying grace of God. It is not that God's people are not able to sin; it is that by His grace they are able not to sin.

We may be tempted, then, through natural desires that are God-given and necessary to our well-being. They are not sinful. Through wrong use, they may indeed become defiled and abnormal, as in the formation of sinful habits and the growth of psychological obsessions. But if properly controlled, all these desires may remain pure and good.

Nor, as we noted earlier, should we fall into the error of thinking that sanctifying grace delivers us from all inner conflict. Temptation involves the struggle of desire against conscience and light—and the struggle can be fierce indeed. But there is no sin unless the choice is made to adopt what is recognized to be an unlawful means of satisfying the desire. "You can never control who knocks on your door. But you do decide who's coming in."

The handling of impure thoughts is a case in point. Our exposure is almost constant. Someone compared the presentation of an impure thought to the exposure of a photographic film. When the impure thought or suggestion is presented, it is possible either to develop the film and retain the picture permanently, or to flood the exposed film with light—the light of Jesus—in which case the picture is washed away.

Nor should we ever think ourselves to be beyond the reach of temptation. Such is perhaps the worst temptation of all. In a perceptive paragraph, Stephen Neill wrote:

> The life of the individual Christian will always be marked by conflict and temptation. Each age, each stage of life, has its own problems, its own pitfalls, its own subtle occasions of failure. It is usually supposed that youth is the period of the most dangerous temptations. I would say rather that it is the time of the most *obvious* temptations. The besetting weakness of middle age is self-complacency and unadventurous acceptance of things as they are. The besetting weakness of old age is an unwillingness to accept the fact of being old, refusal to recognize that one cannot now do the things that one was able to do twenty years ago. With this goes often an inner querulousness about life as God has made it, self-pity, a kind of resentment against the young for being able to do the things one can no longer do oneself, and a consequent refusal to see any good in anything that is new. The existence of all these possibilities of failure is a reminder, if any reminder is still needed, that Christian holiness involves an ever-repeated self-commitment to the exacting demands of the holiness of God in ever-changing situations.[4]

B. Temptations of the Sanctified

A great many temptations are common to all Christians.

They are so obvious as not to need listing. But there are others to which holiness people seem particularly subject. Some of the more obvious may be mentioned here:

1. The temptation to spiritual pride and complacent self-righteousness. Every indication is that it was spiritual pride that brought about the fall of Satan and his angels in the first place. One writer has brutally called it a "God-complex." We must avoid the very appearance of this evil, for it has about it the stench of hell.

2. The temptation to confuse opinions with principles, and incidentals with essentials. It isn't always easy to tell the difference. But we must recognize that not all the opinions of godly men—not even our own!—are eternal principles of right and wrong. To confuse incidentals with essentials is to run the risk of surrendering the essential while making a last-ditch stand for the incidental. Dr. R. T. Williams, Sr., is quoted as saying, "I should hate to choke to death on a piece of ice. I would always think if I could have held on a little longer it would have been gone."

3. The temptation to take an unbalanced view of one's own capabilities. This temptation may take either of two directions. It may lead to a view of one's abilities and service higher than the realities justify. Or it may lead to limiting and crippling one's effectiveness by failing to use to the full and with faith those talents and gifts God has given.

4. The temptation to be unduly critical of differing opinions. Sanctified people are by nature a sure people. They are sure of what God has done for them and they are sure He can do it for all others. But one may be sure without being cocksure, and recognize that certainty does not guarantee infallibility. We must all admit that it is given to none of us to know the whole of God's infinite truth. Intolerance has never been listed as a fruit of the Spirit.

5. The temptation to depreciate what we cannot understand. This is akin to the common tendency to assume that what we cannot fathom is either untrue or unimportant. We need to find a balance between credulity and suspicion, between the "open" mind that swallows everything and the closed mind that will consider nothing new.

6. The temptation to judge others by the light we possess. We tend to be impatient with those who are either immature or not yet established in the sanctifying grace of God. We need always to be reminded that light is given to us to walk in, not to judge others by. Sometimes the Lord must say to us as to Peter, "What is that to you? You must follow me" (John 21:22).

7. The temptation to be unappreciative of the differing abilities of others in the fellowship. In spite of what we know to be true to the contrary, we would still like to have the whole Body of Christ to be foot, or hand, or ear, or eye, or tongue (1 Cor. 12:14-25). We must resist the tendency to pour everybody into the same mold. It is the devil, not God, who is lord of the stereotype.

8. The temptation to insist on having one's own way. This can be a very subtle but real form of pride and egotism. When the judgments of good men differ, it is wrong to insist that things be done a certain way or not at all. This is not much better than the action of the child who picks up his marbles and runs home when he cannot dictate the rules of the game. One prominent layman was overruled on a matter by the board of his church but then graciously accepted the assignment to carry through the project he had opposed. Lo, a big man and a saint!

9. The temptation to substitute standards for sincerity. The sanctified have a built-in horror of moral compromise. Their personal ideals and standards are the highest. But they can drift into legalism in supposing that cleanness of "the

outside of the cup" is the major concern. They may even come to suppose that they receive and retain the favor of God because of what they do *not* do. They forget that holiness is always more than the absence of sin, just as light is more than the absence of darkness.

10. The temptation to substitute sincerity for standards. This is the opposite error and just as fatal. Augustine's dictum to "love the Lord and do as you please" may be accepted if it is correctly interpreted, but it could be the counsel of death and destruction. It is a worldly philosophy that argues, "It doesn't matter what you believe—or do—as long as you are sincere." But sincerity alone is never safe without spiritual standards.

11. The temptation to let good intentions take the place of good actions. Granted that the primary measure of sin and righteousness is the motive or purpose of the heart, a right performance is also vitally important. Blundering goodness can cause almost as much havoc as intentional evil. Some of our greatest problems in the church come from the thoughtless and unconsidered actions of people who "mean well."

12. The temptation to yield to temperamental extremes. While the term *temperament* has been variously used and abused, it actually stands for the inherited emotional climate of our lives. People differ temperamentally, just as they differ physically and in native gifts. The extremes of temperament run all the way from that of the person who reacts to everything with his emotions, to that of the apathetic individual who cannot be stirred at all. Holiness does not instantly change the temperament, but it makes possible the grace to bring it under control.

Temptations of the sanctified, as of all believers, are many and varied. The list is almost endless. Temptations are not sin, but they open the door to sin. But there is one magnificent promise we should write across the bottom of any list of temptations we may draw up: "No temptation has seized you except what is common to man. And God is faithful; he will not let you be tempted beyond what you can bear. But when you are tempted, he will also provide a way out so that you can stand up under it" (1 Cor. 10:13).

C. Overcoming Temptation

Three aspects of overcoming temptation come to light in the accounts of the wilderness temptations of Jesus given in Matthew and Luke.

First, our Lord was spiritually prepared for the contest. He had been anointed by the Holy Spirit at His baptism previously, and had been in prayer. He would later tell His disciples, "Watch and pray so that you will not fall into temptation" (Matt. 26:41).

Stephen Neill reminds us, "It is in the quiet hours that victory is prepared and planned; what happens in the moment of crisis is no more than the revealing of that which has been done or undone, when full opportunity was given to realize our abiding, to confirm our relationship to the living Christ."[5]

Second, Jesus made an immediate refusal. He did not toy with the suggestions offered by Satan—a mistake many of us make to our everlasting sorrow. The victory is more than half won if a person goes into the testing with his mind made up and with his commitments clear.

Third, Jesus made His final appeal to the authority of the Word of God. He met each solicitation of the enemy with a quotation from the Scriptures. When God spoke, there was no debate. "I have hidden your word in my heart that I might not sin against you," the Psalmist said (119:11). Only as we keep our lives fully amenable to the Word of God can we overcome in the hour of temptation.

Always appropriate is the prayer of Annie Hawks in the familiar hymn:

> *I need Thee every hour;*
> *Stay Thou nearby;*
> *Temptations lose their power*
> *When Thou art nigh.*

"It is a beautiful thought," said Cornelius Haggard, "that temptation thus resisted leaves no 'spot or blame' behind, any more than by the shadow of a cloud flying over a beautiful landscape."[6]

II. Sin in the Sanctified Life

One very sensitive question cannot be evaded. It is generally conceded by holiness people that a sanctified person may fall into sin and go back to his old life, even to the point of apostasy and a Christless eternity. That such need never happen must be staunchly affirmed. When it does, it is a total negation of everything the Christian life intends.

A. Total Security

There is total security for every child of God. Christ's promise is true to the last syllable: His sheep do listen to His voice and follow Him, and He does give them eternal life; they shall never perish and no man can snatch them out of His hand (John 10:27-28). It is absolutely true that "neither death nor life, neither angels nor demons, neither the present nor the future, nor any powers, neither height nor depth, nor anything else in all creation, will be able to separate us from the love of God that is in Christ Jesus our Lord" (Rom. 8:38-39).

It would, of course, be wrong to claim these promises for those who have turned away from following the Shepherd or for those whose iniquities have separated them from their

God and whose sins have hidden His face from them (Isa. 59:2). But no believing, obedient child of God need fear for his spiritual security. It is as absolute as the promises of God himself.

We are not concerned here with what is properly called backsliding. Such can and does happen; the prodigal wanders off into the far country and wastes his substance with riotous living (Luke 15:11-31); the "sow that is washed goes back to her wallowing in the mud" (2 Pet. 2:22). The remedy is clear. The prodigal may arise and return to his waiting father; the washing that once cleansed will cleanse again.

B. When the Unexpected Happens

But what happens when a sincere child of God is trapped into sin under the stress of strong temptation and goes down in defeat? Is this the end of his relationship with God through Christ? Is he immediately plunged into depravity, for which the only remedy is a two-step restoration: repentance and justification followed later by consecration and entire sanctification?

There are those who would say yes, perhaps under the influence of Charles G. Finney or by virtue of a theological "hardening of the categories." H. Orton Wiley quotes the response of A. M. Hills to this view: "To hold that a Christian believer in every moral act is as good or bad as he can be, and that the least sudden sin of a warm-hearted Christian plunges him to the level of the worst sinner is too great a tax on credulity to be accepted."[7]

In contrast to such a rigorous and simplistic answer, a long and distinguished line of holiness writers—classic and modern—would reply, "No. It is true that God does not make *allowance* for sin in the Christian life when sin is understood as willful disobedience. But He does make *provision* for it."[8]

There is no real reason to question the conclusion of Myron F. Boyd in his 1969 presidential address to the National Holiness Association in annual convention in St. Louis:

> We believe that even the best of Christians constantly need the atoning blood to cover mistakes, faults, weaknesses, sins of omission or sins of commission. 1 John provides us with clear teaching. God's standard is that the Christian should not sin. God's provision is that if one should sin, he has an Advocate (defense lawyer) with God the Father, even "Jesus Christ the Righteous." The holiness movement has always taught that if a Christian should sin, but comes to God truly repenting, seeking pardon with faith in Christ as his Saviour, he continues as a Christian. We believe that a backslider is one who sins willfully, refuses to confess or seek pardon, and who no longer trusts Christ for his salvation. If a backslider is to enjoy eternal life, he must be born again just as any other sinner.[9]

C. No Allowance; Abundant Provision

As Bishop Boyd observed, the decisive biblical answer to this question is found in 1 John 2:1-2: "My dear children, I write this to you so that you will not sin. But if anybody does sin, we have one who speaks to the Father in our defense—Jesus Christ, the Righteous One. He is the atoning sacrifice for our sins, and not only for ours but also for the sins of the whole world."

The tenor of this statement is clear. God makes no allowance for sin in the Christian life—that is, when sin is understood in the sense of willful disobedience to a known law and is not defined as any shortcoming or deviation from absolute perfection. John puts it directly and unambiguously: "I write this to you so that you will not sin," and the Greek is such as to mean "Not even a single time."

The point is reinforced by the conditional form of the next words: "But *if* anybody does sin . . ." (emphasis mine). It is not *when,* as would be the case were sinning the normal thing. It is clearly the abnormal thing, as a dozen New Testament passages make clear (e.g., John 8:34-36; Rom. 6:1, 15, 22; Gal. 5:16; Heb. 10:26; 1 John 3:8-10).

It is important to notice that these words follow immediately one of the great New Testament affirmations of the cleansed and sanctified life: "If we walk in the light, as he is in the light, we have fellowship with one another, and the blood of Jesus, his Son, purifies us from all sin. If we claim to be without sin [from which we need the cleansing of the Blood], we deceive ourselves and the truth is not in us. If we confess our sins, he is faithful and just and will forgive us our sins and purify us from all unrighteousness. If we claim we have not sinned [as opposed to Rom. 3:23, 'For all have sinned and fall short of the glory of God'], we make him out to be a liar and his word has no place in our lives" (1 John 1:7-10).

The child of God—even the sanctified child of God—is not incapable of sin. Rather, the seed of God in him is *incompatible* with sin. Any sin is a tragic exception, never the accepted rule.

But if the tragedy happens, there is a provision. It is the advocacy of Jesus Christ, the Righteous One, who stands ready to plead our cause with the Father *when* the sin is confessed and renounced.

No ocean liner leaves harbor in the expectation that it will founder and sink before it reaches its destination. No one expects it to sink "every day in word, thought, and deed," as the Westminster Confession says about sin in the Christian life. But it carries a full complement of lifeboats just the same.

C. W. Ruth used to give a simple illustration of this truth. A similar analogy had been used earlier by Beverly Carradine. Every automobile taken out on the road is intended to run on four inflated tires, Ruth said. No driver in his right mind goes out on the highway expecting to have a flat tire. Flat tires are not the rule. Indeed, if a car should have a flat every time it is driven, it is a pretty good sign it needs a set of new tires.

Yet every driver in his right mind carries a spare. He makes provision for what he does not expect. If a flat occurs, there are, of course, two possibilities. One can go on down the road—bumpety bump, bumpety bump, bumpety bump—10, 15, or 20 miles to the next garage or service station. But if he does, he no longer has a simple puncture to deal with. He has a new tire to buy and perhaps a new wheel, and may also have a damaged differential. It takes a major overhaul to get him back on the road. The other alternative is to stop immediately, put on the spare, and go on down the road with only a momentary interruption of the journey.

The application is apparent. Should a Christian fall into a single act of sin—unpremeditated and unexpected—he also has two possibilities. He can go on trying to cover up or rationalize the defeat—bumpety bump, bumpety bump, bumpety bump—to the next revival or camp meeting, 10, 15, or 20 weeks ahead. But if he does, he no longer has one sin to deal with. He has a whole series, including the hypocrisy of covering or rationalizing the first transgression. It takes a major spiritual overhaul to get him back on the road again.

The other alternative is to stop immediately, confess and renounce the sin, receive the advocacy of Christ and the forgiveness of the Father—and go on down the road with only a momentary interruption to the journey. God's provision is gracious and complete. A Christian need never fall. But if he does, he may rise again—sadder but wiser, having learned at least one point where added guardedness is necessary.

A child learns to walk by getting up one more time than he falls down. Here as in other areas of failure, one's attitude toward the failure becomes as important as the failure itself.

In no sense should the apostle John be thought to describe here premeditated or repeated sinning. It is with such that he deals in 3:6-9. He is speaking in chapter 2 of what Thomas Cook called a "surprise sin," when a Christian goes down under the assault of unexpected or unusually severe temptation. But the surprise sin must be dealt with honestly and forthrightly or it opens the door to total and complete backsliding.

Nor is John here considering the case of one who weighs a sin with the calculation, "I can always ask forgiveness and 'get away with it.'" For such presumption there is a rugged and bitter road of repentance. God will not be mocked. There would be good reason to question if one who acts thus really is a child of God at all, much less living in the experience of holiness.

D. A Twofold Danger

Failure so to deal with spiritual defeat results in one of two sad consequences. One is that the defeated one, finding that sin has mastered him contrary to his best expectation, will throw up his arms in surrender, give up his trust in the Savior, and go back to his old life. Many young Christians, who forget or have not been taught the provision of 1 John 2:1-2, do exactly this. Much of the instability among the young may be traced to this cause.

The other consequence is attempting to rationalize away the guilt, to make excuses, and to pretend that nothing is wrong. The result is loss of God's blessing, spiritual sterility, and the onset of either a defeated life or the defensiveness that leads to judgmentalism and legalism. The final end is often a total moral and spiritual breakdown with all the tragedy that follows such a collapse.

Again, it must be said, there can be no delay in dealing with the lapse. John Wesley summed it up in his sermon on Matt. 5:13-16 in the series of discourses on the Sermon on the Mount:

> A believer may fall, and not fall away. He may even fall and rise again. And if he should fall, even into sin, yet this case, dreadful as it is, is not desperate. For "we have an Advo-

cate with the Father, Jesus Christ the righteous; and he is the propitiation for our sins." But let him above all things beware, lest his "heart be hardened by the deceitfulness of sin"; lest he should sink lower and lower, till he wholly falls away, till he become as salt that hath lost its savor.[10]

When restoration comes, it is complete. When the offense that has marred the relationship is taken away, the relationship is restored. Some, to be sure, have argued that if a person loses anything, he loses all. We are reminded that when one falls over a cliff, he never falls just half way; he always hits the bottom. The logic would then require an act of repentance and justifying faith, and a further consecration and moment of full sanctification. The perfect answer is that of Morton Dorsey:

> The Bible does not compare the sanctified life to cliff dwelling, but to matrimony. We are the bride of Christ. It is not the nature of marriage to die from one misunderstanding. A true marriage is strong and resilient. If ever it goes to the grave, that grave will likely result from a long series of little "digs." The relationship of a soul with the Spirit is strong and abiding. He does not depart in a huff the first time we falter or fumble. He rather checks and strives to make the Christian see and correct the error of his way. When correction is made, the case is settled out of court and the relationship remains undamaged.[11]

J. Harold Greenlee paraphrases the key verses we are considering as follows: "I am writing this letter to you to help you not to sin at all. However, if anyone should yield to temptation and commit a sin, he must neither give up his trust in Christ nor ignore what he has done. Jesus is still his intercessor, so let him come to Jesus confessing his sin and trusting Jesus for pardon. Then let him go on walking with Jesus as a child of God."[12]

CHAPTER **6**

THE ALL-SURPASSING POWER OF GOD

No consideration of our human situation would be complete without a look to the future. It is this that Paul addresses in 2 Cor. 4:16-18: "Therefore we do not lose heart. Though outwardly we are wasting away, yet inwardly we are being renewed day by day. For our light and momentary troubles are achieving for us an eternal glory that far outweighs them all. So we fix our eyes not on what is seen, but on what is unseen. For what is seen is temporary, but what is unseen is eternal."

God has left us in these "earthly tents" (5:1) for a purpose. It is that we always cherish the "all-surpassing power" of God, that we do not fall into the deadly trap of self-sufficiency, and that we do not become too attached to what is temporary and which will in its time be dissolved. "We always carry around in our body the death of Jesus," the apostle says, "so that the life of Jesus may also be revealed in our body" (4:10).

Someone composed a worthy prayer: "Father, may I have enough happiness to keep me sweet, enough trials to keep me strong, enough sorrow to keep me human, enough hope to keep me happy, enough failure to keep me humble, enough success to keep me eager, enough faith and courage to banish depression, and enough determination to serve Thee better today than I did yesterday!"

I. MOMENT BY MOMENT

A very dangerous mistake about holiness is to think of sanctifying grace as a possession given to us, sort of a store of something to be used and perhaps periodically replenished. It is rather a relationship with Christ and the Father through the Holy Spirit. As John Seamands writes, "As long as we maintain this intimate relationship, He will keep on cleansing and empowering us from day to day, and the fruit of the Spirit will be evident in our lives." If we allow the relationship to become strained, the Spirit is hindered and we are in spiritual danger.[1]

Such is the obvious point of Christ's great analogy in John 15:1-6: "I am the true vine and my Father is the gardener. He cuts off every branch in me that bears no fruit, while every branch that does bear fruit he trims clean so that it will be even more fruitful. You are already clean because of the word I have spoken to you. Remain in me, and I will remain in you. No branch can bear fruit by itself; it must remain in the vine. Neither can you bear fruit unless you remain in me.

"I am the vine; you are the branches. If a man remains in me and I in him, he will bear much fruit; apart from me you can do nothing. If anyone does not remain in me, he is like a branch that is thrown away and withers; such branches are picked up, thrown into the fire and burned."

As the very life of the branch and its fruitfulness depend on its immediate union with the vine, so does our spiritual life depend on a moment-by-moment relationship with God in the Spirit. This does not suggest fragility or anything tentative, for it is as firm and sure as the promises of God.

No one has seen this more clearly than John Wesley. A persistent theme in his normative work on the doctrine of entire sanctification, *A Plain Account of Christian Perfection* (revised in 1777 when Mr. Wesley was 74 years of age), is emphasis on the moment-by-moment nature of the sanctified life.

"The holiest of men still need Christ," he said. ". . . for He does not give them light, but from moment to moment; the instant He withdraws, all is darkness. They still need Christ as their King; for God does not give them a stock of holiness. But unless they receive a supply every moment, nothing but unholiness would remain."[2]

Even stronger was his statement a little later, "The best of men say, 'Thou art my light, my holiness, my heaven. Through my union with Thee, I am full of light, of holiness, of happiness. But if I were left to myself, I should be nothing but sin, darkness, hell.'"[3]

In his sermon "On Repentance of Believers," Wesley says, "By the same faith we feel the power of Christ every moment resting upon us, whereby alone we are what we are; whereby we are enabled to continue in spiritual life, and without which, notwithstanding all our present holiness, we should be devils the next moment."[4]

As Thomas Cook said, "We teach, not a *state of purity*, but a *maintained condition* of purity, a moment-by-moment obedience and trust. 'The blood of Jesus Christ cleanseth us from all sin' all the time by cleansing us every *Now*."[5]

To think in terms of a "state," as Cook indicated, can easily lead to the holiness equivalent of the Calvinistic doctrine of eternal security. As one observer noted, "One meets sanctified people who claim to have been sanctified for many years, who know little of the Word of God, who show few signs of growth in grace, whose prayer life is feeble, whose zeal has grown cold—but still 'saved and sanctified.'"[6]

There are various ways of describing the moment-by-moment life. Hannah Whitall Smith in her classic, *The Christian's Secret of a Happy Life*, identifies it as "continual surrender" and "continual trust."[7] Albert F. Harper in *Holiness and High Country* speaks of "a maximum openness to the will of God."[8] Oswald Chambers talked about the "totally new relationship" that results from a "few moments of realized transaction, [while] all the rest of the life goes to prove what that transaction means."[9]

Practical ways of bringing this about have been listed by Robert W. Coleman, a listing of sufficient value to be cited in full. He titles it:

SUGGESTIONS FOR DAILY ABIDING

1. Offer yourself fully to Christ anew each morning, breathing this prayer as you awake: "Lord Jesus, I am Thine. Live Thy life through me today."

2. Thank Him for filling you afresh with His Spirit, and often during the day express to Him your praise for His faithfulness.

3. Take time to wait before Him in earnest prayer and reverent reading of the Scripture.

4. Meditate in your quiet moments upon the fact of His indwelling Presence, realizing that the Spirit of God himself, the Holy Spirit, occupies your body, mind, and soul.

5. Confess to Him instantly any unchristlike actions or attitudes the Spirit reveals to you, and accept His cleansing with thanksgiving.

6. Be honest with all men, speak the truth fearlessly, and desire only God's approval.

7. Obey completely the leading of the Spirit, knowing that He never makes a mistake.

8. Rejoice in your adversities, thanking God that you are counted worthy to enter into His sufferings.

9. Look with Christ to some person in need of love, and be His minister.

10. Talk about the wonderful works of God, never boasting of your holiness or accomplishments, but always ready to speak of His.

11. Measure yourself frequently by the Perfection of Christ, and realizing the many failures, omissions, and unimproved opportunities for service which you have unconsciously permitted, resolve to draw closer to Him as He gives you more grace.

12. Commit your way unto the Lord when the day is over, thanking Him for His all-sufficient grace, and close your eyes in the glorious confidence of abiding in Him when you awake.[10]

II. GROWING TO MATURITY

In the theological world, there is a great deal of confusion between purity and maturity, grace and growth. There are those who expect maturity to produce purity; and there are those who expect purity to take the place of maturity. Wiley goes so far as to claim that "failure to distinguish [purity from maturity] lies at the base of practically every objection to entire sanctification."[11]

A. Purity and Maturity

A frequent fallacy is the notion that people may grow into a relationship of grace. On the one hand, this is found in the theory that a person may become a Christian by nurture, or by character development and religious education. It is also found in the widely held view that sanctification is a gradual process in which a believer gains more and more control over his sinful nature and develops more and more the purity of heart the Bible prescribes and promises.

What such views seem to miss is the rather obvious fact that growth does not change the quality or nature of what is growing, but only its quantity or size. If a goat grows, it just becomes a bigger goat. It never grows into a lamb or a sheep.

94

In the same way, both observation and common sense agree that carnal people do not become more saintly by any natural process of growth. If anything, they become more crabbed and carnal. Even when willpower and self-restraint succeed in building a dam against the expression of the sinful nature, more often than not this strategy only increases the flood when the dam breaks.

This is not in any sense to deny that there is growth in Christian graces in the justified life. Any normal Christian experience is a growing experience. What we must see is that there is no way to "grow out" of the carnal mind.

Indeed, growth itself is greatly hindered by the condition within the soul that Paul called "the sinful mind" that "is hostile to God" (Rom. 8:7). Paul describes this sinful mind with the Greek term normally translated "flesh," but which, when contrasted with the Spirit, the NIV translates "sinful nature": "For the sinful nature desires what is contrary to the Spirit, and the Spirit what is contrary to the sinful nature. They are in conflict with each other, so that you do not do what you want" (Gal. 5:17).

It is true that some have interpreted these words to mean that the Spirit restrains the impulses of a carnal heart and keeps the unsanctified Christian from sinful acts he wants to do. An understanding more in keeping with Paul's whole teaching regarding the Christian life is that the sinful condition thus described thwarts the full expression of the purposes of the Spirit. This is parallel to Rom. 7:15, 18, "What I want to do I do not do, . . . For I have the desire to do what is good, but I cannot carry it out." Admittedly, the full situation in Romans 7 is that of an awakened but as yet unconverted man struggling in his own strength to do what his conscience and better judgment tell him he ought to do. But there is a parallel in the experience of the converted person who tries in his own strength to manifest the life of the Spirit.

And those who would make the struggle of Gal. 5:17 and Romans 7 the last word in the Christian life, stop reading too soon. For in Galatians 5, the apostle rejoices that there is a belonging to Christ of such a kind that the "sinful nature" is crucified "with its passions and desires" (v. 24). Likewise, the gloom and defeat of Romans 7 give way to the victory of Romans 8 where Paul exults in the fact that "through Christ Jesus the law of the Spirit of life set me free from the law of sin and death" (v. 2) as light frees one from darkness, as wealth frees him from poverty, and as health from sickness, and life from the corruption of death.

The purity of heart for which the Psalmist prayed—"Create in me a pure heart, O God, and renew a steadfast spirit within me" (Ps. 51:10)—and of which Jesus said, "Blessed are the pure in heart: for they shall see God" (Matt. 5:8, KJV), is not ours to be achieved by repression and force of character. It comes as the expression of sheer grace in the fullness of the Spirit. This, Peter said, is the experience of Pentecost: "God, who knows the heart, showed that he accepted them by giving the Holy Spirit to them, just as he did to us. He made no distinction between us and them, for he purified their hearts by faith" (Acts 15:8-9). The gospel still carries its twofold challenge to "wash your hands, you sinners, and purify your hearts, you double-minded" (James 4:8).

But there is a second fallacy in the consideration of purity and maturity that is almost as deadly as the first. It lies in supposing that purity takes the place of maturity, and that there is nothing beyond the cleansing of the soul except maintaining the "status quo."

Nothing could be farther from the truth. To Peter, the cleansing flame at Pentecost symbolized the purging of his moral nature by the baptism with the Spirit. Yet this, Peter said some 15 years later, was just "the beginning" (Acts 11:15). Grace does not take the place of growth. Rather, it makes growth possible in greater measure than ever before. When the tares are taken out, the wheat may grow unhindered.

B. The Wesleyan Paradox

This is what Daniel Steele called "the Wesleyan paradox."[12] It is to the effect that sanctification is both the work of a moment and a growing experience. Holiness is both perfect and progressive, critical and continuing. Paul states this in 2 Cor. 7:1, "Since we have these promises, dear friends, let us purify ourselves from everything that contaminates body and spirit, perfecting holiness out of reverence for God."

In this verse the apostle reminds us of the promises to which we are heirs. Ours is the assurance that the Lord Almighty is our Heavenly Father and that we are His sons and daughters (2 Cor. 6:16-18). In view of this, we are to cleanse ourselves from all filthiness of the flesh and spirit (KJV).

This is a "crisis" cleansing. It is the work of a moment. It is the purging of the soul from sinful dispositions and tendencies. Its result, as has been said, is that "everything inside is on God's side." But the moment of cleansing is not the end. It is the beginning of a lifelong task of "perfecting holiness out of reverence for God." "Perfecting holiness is a progressive work."[13]

The contrast between the two sides of the paradox is much more clear in the Greek New Testament than in the English translations. The exhortation to "purify ourselves" refers to something completed and entire, something to be done and finished. The directive to be "perfecting holiness" describes an ongoing process. Literally, "perfecting" holiness is bringing it to maturity.

We have a very practical example of a similar paradox in the realm of human experience. The love we experience in human relationships may be pure—excluding all competing affections. Yet it may grow year by year, always becoming more mature and more secure. In fact, love that does not grow will eventually die or turn to outright aversion.

To insist on the momentary cleansing and ignore the progressive growth in grace is to risk a shallow, emotional, unrealistic, and immature religious life. To urge the progressive aspects of the sanctified life and deny or ignore the need for a definite act of commitment and cleansing is to find the futility of trying to build without a foundation. Both sides are essential; we cannot have one without the other any more than we can run on one leg or row a boat with one oar.

Both are constant elements in the teaching of Scripture. Sanctification, holiness, purity, fullness, the finished work of Christ are too clearly taught to be convincingly denied. But so are the incentives to moral effort—growth, achievement, and the need to work out in every area of life the salvation God is working in us. John Allen Knight writes:

> To emphasize the crisis to the neglect of process can only produce moral insensitivity and stagnation, spiritual infantilism, and a lack of real Christian growth. Or it may create introspective, if not legalistic, Christians whose primary concern is to *preserve* the holiness they already "possess," rather than living creatively and abundantly in the life which they have come to share in Christ. . . . Consequently, *discipleship is undercut.* [14]

One thing worse than the desire to be "carried to the skies on flowery beds of ease" is the wish to go there in a crib!

So there is no smugness, no complacency about true holiness. Just the opposite is the case. The satisfying feeling of "having arrived" is certain evidence that the journey has not yet started. What we are given is not "a place of holiness" but "a highway . . . called the Way of Holiness" (Isa. 35:8). A highway is not somewhere to park; it is a road to travel. Entire sanctification is not the goal but the gateway, not the destination but the point of beginning.

Paul tells us that one of the purposes of the varied ministries in the Body of Christ is so "we all . . . become mature, attaining to the whole measure of the fullness of Christ. Then we will no longer be infants, tossed back and forth. . . . Instead, speaking the truth in love, we will in all things grow up into him who is the Head, that is, Christ" (Eph. 4:13-15).

So while we cannot *grow into* grace, either of the new birth or of heart holiness, we can and must *grow in* "the grace and knowledge of our Lord and Savior Jesus Christ" (2 Pet. 3:18). Since our goal is "the whole measure of the fullness of Christ," not even "the sky is the limit." To become more and more like Christ in every expression as well as impulse, in word and deed as well as motive—this must be the high and holy aim of every Christian worthy of the name in any degree. As we saw earlier, perfection as commonly conceived is *impossible* as a standard; by the same token, it is *inescapable* as an ideal.

God has made us partakers of His divine nature, freeing us from the corruption that is in the world through lust (2 Pet. 1:4, KJV). This is purity, the work of grace. He commands us, then, to "make every effort" to add to our faith the graces of goodness, knowledge, self-control, perseverence, godliness, brotherly kindness, and love (2 Pet. 1:5-7). For if we "possess these qualities," they will keep us "from being ineffective and unproductive in [our] knowledge of our Lord Jesus Christ. But if anyone does not have them, he is nearsighted and blind, and has forgotten that he has been cleansed from his past sins" (2 Pet. 1:8-9).

C. Our Human Obligation

It should have become clear that the responsibility for growth is part of our human obligation. One of the holiness fathers, Isaiah Reid, wrote a series of contrasts between grace and growth. He stated that "growth is but the co-operation of the human spirit, and belongs to the man side of the question of salvation. Growth has reference always to the exercise of any of these unto more godliness. Growth is never into, but always in, grace." He gives a series of contrasts:

Grace is of God; growth is of man.

Grace is conferred; growth is commanded.

Grace is a favor; growth is a duty.

Grace is administered; growth is attained.

Grace is before growth; for a thing that is not, cannot grow.

Grace is the unmerited helpfulness of God administered in love. Growth is the enlarging of the ways of God's helpfulness within us, and the exercise of what is given in such ways that there is continual increase. . . .

Grace is like the air we breathe, or the water for which we thirst—all good of themselves, all free; but all to no avail unless appropriated and individually used.

Growth refers first to this personal appropriation, and next to the enlargement that comes from so doing.[15]

To keep clearly in mind the nature and necessity of spiritual growth will save us from unrealistic expectation in purity of what only comes through maturity. It is easy to confuse direction with distance. The moment of grace in our lives represents a change in direction. It does not mean that the newly converted or newly sanctified will find himself instantly where the saint of 40 years ought to be—but, sadly, often is not. In this sense, there is no instant sainthood.

D. How We Grow

This does not mean that spiritual growth proceeds at the same rate in every individual—that each one who has been sanctified for 10 years will be exactly as far along as every other person who has been sanctified the same length of time. There are differences of capacity, temperament, and circumstance that influence the developing graces of the Christian life. We do not all grow at uniform rates physically or mentally. Neither do we all grow at the same rate spiritually and morally.

Nor do we mature at the same rate in all the areas of personal life. Various aspects of our personalities may grow or mature at quite different rates. One may be mature in capacities for service, and very immature, for instance, in the ability to understand conflicts within himself. A believer may even be stunted emotionally and suffer various psychosomatic disorders, just as he may suffer from physical injury or disease. In addition, one aspect of partial immaturity may be failure to recognize the fact that God has not promised immunity from ills of this sort any more than He has from liability to physical sickness or accident.

When we become aware of the fact that we are not expected to be finished products but people in the process of becoming all God wants us to be, it can lift an intolerable load from us. We are free then to be what we are without abnormal stretching to try to be at once what we are going to be eventually. A whimsical gospel song proclaims that

> He's still workin' on me
> To make me what I ought to be;
> It took Him just a week to make
>   The moon and the stars,
> The sun and the earth,
>   And Jupiter and Mars.
> How loving and patient He must be,
> 'Cause He's still workin' on me. [16]

Growth also is largely unconscious. Preoccupation with progress may delay the very progress desired. One has only to recall how focusing attention on getting to sleep makes sleep more elusive and how determination to stay awake makes sleep more irresistible! We never achieve healthful physical or emotional growth by going around with our fingers on our pulses, any more than we grow sturdy plants by pulling them up every few days to see how the roots are doing.

We do not grow by work and worry any more than we are sanctified by struggle. Jesus bids us, "See how the lilies of the field grow. They do not labor or spin" (Matt. 6:28), and most of the growth is underground, quite out of sight.

Growth is a product of the vitality of the organism. We grow spiritually by cultivating the principles of the spiritual life. We can no more cause a plant or a tree to grow by direct effort than we can cause the sun to rise or the tide to come in. We help the plant or the tree to grow by feeding it, watering it, pruning it, and in general nourishing its life.

And we must never forget that there is what has been called "that inner tug, the constant tension between the level on which [we] are now living and the level toward which [we know we] should move."[17] "There is a constant tug to come up higher. Without this tug or tension, our lives tend to level off and to become a more or less monotonous routine."[18] To lose the growing edge and to be satisfied with what we have already mastered, or to "polish the past," is to run the risk of spiritual death.

Psychologists have given us many excellent lists of the marks of maturity, a number of which apply to the mature Christian. To examine them to any extent would demand a volume in itself.

One frequently mentioned mark of maturity is of particular concern to us here. It is the capacity for self-acceptance, an honest evaluation of our own strengths and weaknesses. This is summarized in Paul's injunction in connection with his great appeal to Christian consecration (Rom. 12:1-2): "By the grace given me I say to every one of you: Do not think of yourself more highly than you ought, but rather think of yourself with sober judgment, in accordance with the measure of faith God has given you" (v. 3).

The point has often been made that there is a proper self-love that serves as the model and measure of our love for others. This does not deny the balancing truth of self-denial, a crucifixion of carnal expressions of self. It does point up the need for the capacity expressed in the famed prayer of Reinhold Niebuhr: "Lord, give us the courage to change what can be changed, the patience to bear what cannot be changed, and the wisdom to know the difference."

Only by coming to such self-acceptance are we really able to accept others with all their shortcomings and idiosyncrasies. Only so can we truly accept responsibility without "passing the buck." Self-acceptance frees one to express himself and his emotions in constructive and wholesome ways. Through self-acceptance one can profit by criticism without defensiveness. A self-accepting person doesn't always have to be right.

Perhaps it would suffice simply to add that Christian maturity in its basic expression is Christlikeness. And Christlikeness is best described in that sparkling list of qualities Paul called "the fruit of the Spirit . . . love, joy, peace, patience, kindness, goodness, faithfulness, gentleness and self-control" (Gal. 5:22-23).

These are "fruit" in contrast to the preceding "works" of the flesh (vv. 19-21). A "work" is an act over and done. "Fruit" is an organic concept and involves bud, blossom, forming fruit, and finally the mature, ripe fruit. To become more mature spiritually is to be more loving, joyous, serene, patient, kind, good, faithful, gentle, and self-controlled. Here is a lifetime program of progress for each of us.

There is said to be an epitaph in a little Swiss cemetery near the Matterhorn set on the grave of a famous mountaineer who lost his life on the mountainside: "He died climbing."

Lot's wife looked back and became a pillar of salt. A Christian who looks back, it has been said, tends to become a pillar of starch!

103

A worthy prayer for us all is voiced by Frances Ridley Havergal:

Deepen all Thy work, O Master,
*   Strengthen every downward root,*
Only do Thou ripen faster,
*   More and more, Thy pleasant fruit.*
Purge me, prune me, self abase,
Only let me grow in grace.

Jesus, grace for grace outpouring,
*   Show me ever greater things;*
Raise me higher, sunward soaring,
*   Mounting as on eagle wings.*
By the brightness of Thy face,
Jesus, let me grow in grace.

Let me then be always growing,
*   Never, never standing still;*
Listening, learning, better knowing
*   Thee and Thy most blessed will.*
Till I reach Thy holy place,
Daily let me grow in grace. [19]

III. AGING

The fact of aging in human experience is a constant re-minder of the limitations of this mortal existence. Even so, it isn't so bad, as someone said, when you consider the alternative!

Dennis the Menace looked at his elderly neighbor crit-ically: "You're getting old, Mr. Wilson," he said. Then sensing that he had said the wrong thing, he quickly added, "But there's a lot of that going around these days!"

Indeed there is—more than ever. The fastest growing age-group in the United States today is composed of those 65 years of age and older. The advances and availability of medical science and somewhat better living conditions for many have dramatically extended the span of human life on this earth.

To live is to grow old. The only other option is one we all put off as long as possible. We can do nothing whatever about the fact of aging. We can control the way we face it.

Aging can be a grim and bitter experience for those who live without faith in the God and Father of our Lord Jesus Christ. But those who have committed their lives to Christ face the fact of aging sustained by the promises of God. Theirs is a firm foundation; as the hymn writer put it:

> E'en down to old age all My people shall prove
> My sov'reign, eternal, unchangeable love.

The righteous, declares the Psalmist, "Will still bear fruit in old age, they will stay fresh and green" (92:14). Isaiah echoes God's promise: "Even to your old age and gray hairs I am he, I am he who will sustain you. I have made you and I will carry you; I will sustain you and I will rescue you" (46:4). In the age of the Spirit, says Joel, while the young see visions, "your old men will dream dreams" (2:28).

Jesus promised that the Holy Spirit as the divine helper "will be with you forever" (John 14:16), and said of himself, "Surely I am with you always, to the very end of the age" (Matt. 28:20). Paul's great affirmation was, "Therefore we do not lose heart. Though outwardly we are wasting away, yet inwardly we are being renewed day by day. For our light and momentary troubles are achieving for us an eternal glory that far outweighs them all" (2 Cor. 4:16-17).

A. The Changes Age Brings

Yet aging brings its changes and the Christian must be prepared to cope with them. There is the sad paradox that the very society that has extended the length of life and multiplied the numbers of the old is at the same time a society that glorifies youth and tends to discard the elderly. Old age becomes for many a time of loneliness. Life tends to push the elderly to the side of the stream while the current flows on at ever swifter pace. Friends and loved ones are taken and there is "change and decay in all about."

The years bring an inevitable decline of physical powers. Age increases the liability to illness. There are diseases that prey on the aged to which most younger people are immune.

Modern society tends to measure people by their possessions. "How much is he worth?" always means "How much money or property does he have?" But age is usually a period of declining productivity and fewer possessions.

There is an increase in the stress life imposes just at the time when natural powers of resistance are at a lower ebb. Two American psychiatrists (Doctors Thomas Holmes and Richard Rahe) have listed the top 10 stressful life-changes to which people are exposed. While all may occur at any stage of life, 4 of the 10 are most likely to happen in later years: retirement; the death of close family members; personal illness; and most severe of all, the death of husband or wife.

Much of what happens to us we can do nothing about. This we must learn to accept in dependence on the unfailing grace of God. But some of the negatives that come with aging can be turned to positives. Each stage of life has its liabilities, and each has its assets.

Our years should bring us better perspective. As we come closer to the gateway to eternity, the material and earthly things behind us should decrease in size and importance. We should strive for more serenity. We should have learned that worry and anxiety never really help. We should grow more tolerant, more ready to forgive, more aware of the times we could rightfully have said, "There, but for the grace of God, go I." Our experience of the adequacy of God's grace in years past should strengthen our confidence in the sufficiency of His grace for the years ahead.

B. Aging as Bane or Blessing

While we can't change the fact of aging, there are some things we can do to ease its burdens, for ourselves and others. Although we can't do anything about growing older, we can do something about the kind of older persons we become.

Swiss psychiatrist, Paul Tournier, noted that generally speaking old people can be "divided into two well-defined categories, with few intermediate shades." One of these he described as the "awful old people, selfish, demanding, domineering, bitter. They are always grumbling and criticizing everybody. If you go and see them, they upbraid you for not having come sooner; they misjudge your best intentions, and the conversation becomes a painful conflict."

But then, there are the

> wonderful old people, kind, sociable, radiant with peace. Troubles and difficulties only seem to make them grow still further in serenity. They make no claims, and it is a pleasure to see them and to help them. They are grateful, and even astonished, that things are done for them, and that they are still loved. They read, they improve their minds, they go for quiet walks, they are interested in everything, they are prepared to listen to anyone.[20]

E. Stanley Jones in his book *Growing Spiritually* gives an incisive list of advices for making the later years we spend in these earthen vessels more worthwhile:

1. Don't retire. Change your occupation.
2. Learn something new every day.
3. Set yourself to be gracious to somebody every day.
4. Don't let yourself grow negative; be positive.
5. Look around you to find something for which to be grateful every day.
6. Now that your bodily activities are slowing down, let your spiritual activities increase.
7. Keep laying up as the years come and go "the good store"—the depository of every thought, motive, action, attitude, which we drop into the subconscious mind.[21]

107

With God's help, age may make us better, not bitter. The greatest gift we can leave those who follow is a radiant and victorious old age. Science has added years to our lives. It is up to us to add life to our years.

True happiness means acceptance of one's age. The adult must accept the fact that he is no longer a child. The one advanced in years must give up the goals of active life. Years of retirement may be either a magnificent experience or a bitter trial. The difference is not in outward circumstances. Those who complain about their retirement are usually the very people who used to complain about their work.

C. The Young in Heart

There is always the fact that an older body may house a spirit perennially young. "Though outwardly we are wasting away, yet inwardly we are being renewed day by day" (2 Cor. 4:16). In this sense, age is a quality of mind. The eloquent General Douglas MacArthur, at age 76 and five years into retirement from active service with the armed forces, said to a group of businessmen in Los Angeles:

> You are as young as your faith, as old as your doubt; as young as your confidence, as old as your fear; as young as your hope, as old as your despair. In the central place of every heart there is a recording chamber; so long as it receives messages of beauty, hope, cheer and courage, so long are we young. When the wires are all down and your heart is covered with the snows of pessimism and the ice of cynicism, then and then only are you grown old.[22]

D. "On the Verge of Life"

In the end, the measure of life is not what we must leave behind us. It is what we are and that to which we go. When, in St. Paul's words, "To live is Christ," then "to die is gain" (Phil. 1:21). Christ is not only the Alpha but also the Omega; He is not only the beginning but also the end.

I know not when I go, nor where,
From this familiar scene;
But Christ is here, and Christ is there,
And all the way between. [23]

When the time of our departure is at hand, we do not go down toward the sunset. We move toward the dawning of eternal day. John Wesley commented on Paul's words in 2 Tim. 1:3 as the apostle was facing martyrdom: "One who stands *on the verge of life* is much refreshed by the remembrance of his predecessors, to whom he is going."[24]

For a Christian, in Thomas Wolfe's hauntingly beautiful words, "To lose the earth you know, for greater knowing; to lose the life you have, for greater life; to leave the friends you loved, for greater loving; to find a land more kind than home, more large than earth"[25] this is not losing and leaving; this is finding and gaining.

Of those who have entered the larger room in their Father's mansion, let us remember that "God has not taken them from us; He has hidden them in His heart that they may be closer to ours."[26] Leslie Weatherhead said:

> Those whom we foolishly call the dead are far more alive than we are. They are beyond the fog and dirt and clouds of the smoky earth-cities. They are out on the great mountains of experience, with the infinite sky above them and the never fading sunshine round about them; there, where the great winds blow, and men breathe an air we have never known and look upon a loveliness we have never seen.[27]

IV. THE FINAL RESTORATION

Paul closes the memorable fourth chapter of 2 Corinthians with one of his great summary statements that carry us beyond the limitations of this life into the realm eternal: "For our light and momentary troubles are achieving for us an eternal glory that far outweighs them all. So we fix our eyes not on what is seen, but on what is unseen. For what is seen is temporary, but what is unseen is eternal" (vv. 17-18). This, in Gerit Berkouwer's words, is the familiar contrast between the "already" and the "not yet"; between the "now" and "later."[28]

It makes all the difference in the world when the years do not bring us closer to death but nearer to God. The great promise of redemption is that while our mortal bodies are destined for the dust, the dust is not their end. In a way and manner we cannot comprehend, they are destined to rise again not in the image of the earthly but in "the likeness of the man from heaven" (1 Cor. 15:49).

The Scottish theologian, John Baillie, observed that "not even the most learned philosopher or theologian knows what it is going to be like. But there is one thing which the simplest Christian knows—he knows it is going to be all right."[29] As Richard Baxter wrote:

> My knowledge of that life is small,
>   The eye of faith is dim;
> But 'tis enough that Christ knows all,
>   And I shall be with Him. [30]

Really, about all we know of the resurrection life is provided in the glimpse we have of the risen Redeemer and what Paul tells us in 1 Corinthians 15. Christ's resurrection body is the paradigm of ours: "Our citizenship is in heaven. And we eagerly await a Savior from there, the Lord Jesus Christ, who, by the power that enables him to bring everything under his control, will transform our lowly bodies so that they will be like his glorious body" (Phil. 3:20-21); "Dear friends, now we are children of God, and what we will be has not yet been made known. But we know that when he appears, we shall be like him, for we shall see him as he is" (1 John 3:2).

Paul's teaching in 1 Corinthians 15 is based on the fact of Christ's resurrection as the sole guarantee of our faith:

"Christ has indeed been raised from the dead, the first-fruits of those who have fallen asleep. . . .

"When you sow, you do not plant the body that will be, but just a seed, perhaps of wheat or of something else. But God gives it a body as he has determined, and to each kind of seed he gives its own body. . . .

"So will it be with the resurrection of the dead. The body that is sown is perishable, it is raised imperishable; it is sown in dishonor, it is raised in glory; it is sown in weakness, it is raised in power; it is sown a natural body, it is raised a spiritual body. . . .

"And just as we have borne the likeness of the earthly man, so shall we bear the likeness of the man from heaven. . . .

"Listen, I tell you a mystery: We will not all sleep, but we will all be changed—in a flash, in the twinkling of an eye, at the last trumpet. For the trumpet will sound, the dead will be raised imperishable, and we will be changed. For the perishable must clothe itself with the imperishable, and the mortal with immortality. When the perishable has been clothed with the imperishable, and the mortal with immortality, then the saying that is written will come true: 'Death has been swallowed up in victory.'

'Where, O death, is your victory?
Where, O death, is your sting?'

The sting of death is sin, and the power of sin is the law. But thanks be to God! He gives us the victory through our Lord Jesus Christ.

"Therefore, my dear brothers, stand firm. Let nothing move you. Always give yourselves fully to the work of the Lord, because you know that your labor in the Lord is not in vain" (vv. 20, 37-38, 42-44, 49, 51-58).

REFERENCE NOTES

INTRODUCTION

1. Harold B. Kuhn in Kenneth Geiger, comp., *Insights into Holiness* (Kansas City: Beacon Hill Press, 1962), 255.

2. "John Wesley and Creative Synthesis," *Preacher's Magazine,* Vol. 59, No. 3 (March, April, May, 1984), 48.

3. Cf. Larry Hart in *Christianity Today,* Vol. 28, No. 7 (April 20, 1984), 51.

4. H. A. Baldwin, *Holiness and the Human Element* (Kansas City: Beacon Hill Press, 1952 reprint), 5.

5. Leon and Mildred Chambers, *Holiness and Human Nature* (Kansas City: Beacon Hill Press of Kansas City, 1975), 10.

6. Cf. Robert E. Cushman, *Practical Divinity* (Nashville: Abingdon Press, 1983), 213-15.

CHAPTER 1. THIS TREASURE

1. Stephen Neill, *Christian Holiness* (New York: Harper and Brothers, Publishers, 1960), 114.

2. H. Orton Wiley, *Christian Theology* (Kansas City: Beacon Hill Press, 1940), 2:231.

3. Richard Quebedeaux, *The Young Evangelicals: Revolution in Orthodoxy* (New York: Harper and Row, Publishers, n.d.), 38.

4. *Oswald Chambers, His Life and Work,* foreword by Dinsdale T. Young (London: Marshall, Morgan and Scott, Ltd., 1959), 167.

5. Harriet Auber; quoted by William M. Greathouse, "Romans," *Search the Scriptures* (Kansas City: Nazarene Publishing House, n.d.), 6:35.

6. Cf. Albert C. Outler, *Evangelism in the Wesleyan Spirit* (Nashville: Tidings, 1971), 68—Outler's characterization of some of the holiness people in the Methodist church in the early part of the century.

7. Quoted from A. Skevington Wood, *Life by the Spirit* (Grand Rapids: Zondervan Publishing House, 1963), 30.

8. See Esther Kerr Rusthoi's lines, "When We See Christ," *Worship in Song,* No. 257.

CHAPTER 2. EARTHEN VESSELS

1. Cf. Robert K. Johnston, "What Is the Major Shift in Theological Focus?" *Christianity Today*, Vol. 28, No. 2 (Feb. 3, 1984), 78-79.

2. Written question submitted in a holiness seminar in Kansas City.

3. Wiley, *Christian Theology*, 2:499.

4. Cf. Allister Smith, *The Ideal of Perfection* (London: Oliphants, Ltd., 1963), 69-90.

5. C. A. Simpson, *Interpreter's Bible*, Geo. Buttrick, ed. (Nashville: Abingdon Press, 1952), 1:494, exeg.

6. Francis Brown, S. R. Driver, and Charles A. Briggs, *Hebrew and English Lexicon of the Old Testament* (New York: Houghton Mifflin Co., 1907), ad loc.

7. W. E. Vine, *An Expository Dictionary of New Testament Words* (London: Oliphants, Ltd., n.d.), 4:54.

8. William F. Arndt and F. Wilbur Gingrich, *A Greek-English Lexicon of the New Testament and Other Early Christian Literature* (Chicago: University of Chicago Press, 1957), ad loc.

9. Wilber Dayton, "Heart," *Beacon Dictionary of Theology*, Richard S. Taylor, ed. (Kansas City: Beacon Hill Press of Kansas City, 1983), 249.

10. Vincent Taylor, *The Apostolic Gospel*, 8-9; quoted by A. Skevington Wood, *The Burning Heart: John Wesley, Evangelist* (Grand Rapids: Wm. B. Eerdmans Publishing Co., 1967), 234.

11. Harold O. J. Brown, *The Protest of a Troubled Protestant* (New Rochelle, N.Y.: Arlington House, 1969), 171. Cf. Wiley, *Christian Theology*, 2:95.

12. "Articles of Faith," Article V, Constitution of the Church of the Nazarene, *Manual: Church of the Nazarene* (Kansas City: Nazarene Publishing House, 1980), 27, emphasis added.

13. John Wesley, *Works*, 9:274-75; quoted in *Insights into Holiness*, Kenneth Geiger, comp., 285.

14. Reinhold Neibuhr, *The Nature and Destiny of Man*, 1:251; quoted by George Allen Turner, *The Vision Which Transforms* (Kansas City: Beacon Hill Press of Kansas City, 1964), 279.

15. Henry Drummond, *The Greatest Thing in the World* (London: Collins' Cleartype Press, n.d.), 38.

16. T. A. Hegre, *The Cross and Sanctification* (Minneapolis, Minn.: Bethany Fellowship, Inc., 1960), 158.

CHAPTER 3. IMPERFECT PERFECTION

1. *The American College Dictionary* (New York: Random House, 1953), 900; a total of 17 different meanings are listed.

2. *Webster's New World Dictionary of the American Language,* revised (New York: Popular Library, 1973), 424.

3. *The New Grolier Webster International Dictionary of the English Language* (New York: Grolier, 1976), 703.

4. Albert C. Outler, *John Wesley,* 10; quoted by Wood, *Burning Heart,* 43.

5. John Wesley, *Letters* (To Dorothy Furly, Sept. 15, 1762), 4:188; quoted by Frederick Dale Bruner, *A Theology of the Holy Spirit* (Grand Rapids: Wm. B. Eerdmans Publishing Co., 1970), 329.

6. Jack Ford, *In the Steps of John Wesley* (Kansas City: Nazarene Publishing House, 1968), 254.

7. Wesley, *Works* (Kansas City: Nazarene Publishing House, n.d.), 11:417.

8. Wesley, *Letters,* 5:204; quoted by J. Baines Atkinson, *The Beauty of Holiness* (London: The Epworth Press, 1953), 118.

9. Cf. Mildred Bangs Wynkoop, *A Theology of Love: The Dynamic of Wesleyanism* (Kansas City: Beacon Hill Press of Kansas City, 1972), 294.

10. Cf. William Barclay, *The New Testament: A New Translation,* 2 vols. (London: Collins, 1969), 2:319.

11. Francis Schaeffer, *True Spirituality* (Wheaton, Ill.: Tyndale House Publishers, 1971), 96.

12. Cf. Wynkoop, *Theology of Love,* 227 ff.

13. Charles Hodge, *Systematic Theology,* 2:185; quoted in *Further Insights into Holiness,* Kenneth Geiger, comp. (Kansas City: Beacon Hill Press, 1963), 167.

14. J. C. Ryle, *A Call to Holiness* (Grand Rapids: Baker Book House, 1976), 2.

15. Daniel Steele, *Milestone Papers,* 127; quoted by Charles Newman Curtis, *An Epoch in the Spiritual Life* (New York: Eaton and Mains, 1908), 41.

16. Cf. W. T. Purkiser, *Conflicting Concepts of Holiness* (Kansas City: Beacon Hill Press, 1953), 45-56.

17. Archibald Hunter, *P. T. Forsyth: Per Crucem ad Lucem* (Naperville, Ill.: SCM Book Club, 1974), 57.

18. Cf. the treatment by Delbert R. Rose in *Insights into Holiness,* Geiger, comp., 107 ff.

19. W. Curry Mavis, *The Psychology of Christian Experience* (Grand Rapids: Zondervan Publishing House, 1963), 62.

20. Ibid.

21. Ibid.

22. Ibid., 68-69.

23. Dennis F. Kinlaw, William C. Cessna, Gilbert K. James, *The Sanctified Life* (Wilmore, Ky.: The Seminary Press, 1968), 10.

Chapter 4. Some Problem Areas

1. Malcolm Jeeves, *Psychology and Christianity: The View Both Ways* (Downers Grove, Ill.: InterVarsity Press, 1976), 108-9.

2. Chambers, *Holiness and Human Nature*, 21.

3. Elizabeth Cheney, 19th-century writer.

4. Cf. Baldwin, *Holiness and the Human Element*, 22.

5. Olin Alfred Curtis, *The Christian Faith* (Grand Rapids: Kregel Publications, 1956 reprint; first publication, 1903), 393.

6. George Macdonald in *An Anthology*, compiled by C. S. Lewis (Garden City, N.Y.: Doubleday and Co., a Dolphin Book; 1947 copyright by Macmillan), 46-47.

7. Quoted, W. Curry Mavis, *The Holy Spirit in the Christian Life* (Grand Rapids: Baker Book House, 1977), 22.

8. Cf. the excellent treatment in Chambers, *Holiness and Human Nature*, 21.

9. Kinlaw, Cessna, and James, *Sanctified Life*, 12.

10. Quoted by Albert Lown, *Mastering Our Moods* (Kansas City: Beacon Hill Press of Kansas City, 1967), n.p.

11. Quoted in *Herald of Holiness*, Vol. 49, No. 52 (Feb. 22, 1961), 12.

12. Norman Snaith, *Hymns of the Temple* (London: SCM Press, Ltd., 1951), 82.

Chapter 5. Temptation and Sin

1. The NIV with its translation "evil desire" is totally wrong. If temptation comes only from "evil desire," Jesus could never have been tempted.

2. Cf. Victor E. Frankl, *Man's Search for Meaning: An Introduction to Logotherapy* (New York: Washington Square Press, 1966), 175.

3. Wiley, *Christian Theology*, 2:500.

4. Neill, *Christian Holiness*, 104-5.

5. Ibid., 126

6. In Geiger, *Further Insights into Holiness,* 206-7.

7. A. M. Hills, *Fundamental Christian Theology,* 2:253; quoted by Wiley, *Christian Theology,* 2:456.

8. Included here would be such classic writers as Daniel Steele, Thomas Cook, G. D. Watson, S. A. Keen, Hannah W. Smith, Beverly Carradine, Major Allister Smith; and such more recent authors as J. B. Chapman, Samuel Young, John Allen Knight, Harold Greenlee, Robert W. Coleman, William S. Deal, Albert F. Harper, and Richard S. Taylor.

9. Unpublished mimeographed manuscript.

10. John Wesley, *Sermons on Several Occasions,* 2 vols. (New York: Lane and Scott, 1852), 1:214.

11. Morton Dorsey, in *Projecting Our Heritage,* Myron F. Boyd, comp. (Kansas City: Beacon Hill Press of Kansas City, 1969), 128.

12. J. Harold Greenlee, in *Good News,* April-June, 1971, 40.

CHAPTER 6. THE ALL-SURPASSING POWER OF GOD

1. John T. Seamands, *On Tiptoe with Love* (Kansas City: Beacon Hill Press of Kansas City, 1972), 85.

2. John Wesley, *A Plain Account of Christian Perfection* (Kansas City: Beacon Hill Press of Kansas City, 1966 reprint), 71.

3. Ibid., 82-83.

4. Wesley, *Sermons on Several Occasions,* 1:123.

5. Thomas Cook, *New Testament Holiness* (London: The Epworth Press, 1952), 43; cf. Wynkoop, *Theology of Love,* 252.

6. *The Doctrine of Holiness in These Times* (Arlington Heights, Ill.: Conservative Baptist Association of America, 1952), 62.

7. Hannah Whitall Smith, *The Christian's Secret of a Happy Life* (Westwood, N.J.: Fleming H. Revell Company, 1952, reprint), 32.

8. A. F. Harper, *Holiness and High Country* (Kansas City: Beacon Hill Press of Kansas City, 1964), 135.

9. Oswald Chambers, *If Thou Wilt Be Perfect . . . Talks on Spiritual Philosophy* (London: Simpkin Marshall, Ltd., 1949 reprint), 89.

10. Robert W. Coleman, *The Spirit and the Word* (Wilmore, Ky.: Asbury Theological Seminary, 1965), 64. Used by permission.

11. Wiley, *Christian Theology,* 2:506.

12. Daniel Steele, *Milestone Papers* (Kansas City: Beacon Hill Press abridgement, n.d.), 40.

13. Ibid., 107.

14. John Allen Knight, *The Holiness Pilgrimage: Reflections on*

the Life of Holiness (Kansas City: Beacon Hill Press of Kansas City, 1973), 60.

15. Isaiah Reid, *How They Grow,* 10-11; quoted by Roy S. Nicholson, *The Arminian Emphasis* (Owosso, Mich: Owosso College, n.d.), 76.

16. Joel Hemphill. Copyright by Benson Music Co., Nashville. Used by permission.

17. T. B. Maston, *Why Live the Christian Life?* (Nashville: Thomas Nelson Inc., 1974), 134.

18. Ibid., 179.

19. Quoted by J. Paul Taylor, *Holiness the Finished Foundation* (Winona Lake, Ind.: Light and Life Press, 1963), 198-99.

20. Paul Tournier, *Learn to Grow Old* (New York: Harper and Row, Publishers, 1972), 118.

21. E. Stanley Jones, *Growing Spiritually* (New York: Abingdon Press, 1953), 315.

22. Quoted by Robert Schuller in *Move Ahead with Possibility Thinking* (Garden City, N.Y.: Doubleday and Company, Inc., 1967), 116.

23. Credited to Annie Johnson Flint.

24. John Wesley, *Explanatory Notes upon the New Testament* (Naperville, Ill.: Alec R. Allenson, Inc., 1958 reprint), 788.

25. Thomas Wolfe, *You Can't Go Home Again,* 743.

26. Anonymous quotation in Emily Gardiner Neal, *In the Midst of Life* (New York: Morehouse-Barlow Co., 1963), 5.

27. Leslie Weatherhead, *Prescription for Anxiety* (New York: Abingdon Press, 1956), 120.

28. Exact source unavailable.

29. John Baillie, *Christian Devotion,* 113; quoted in Elton Trueblood, *The Lord's Prayers* (New York: Harper and Row, 1965), 92.

30. Richard Baxter, quoted in Clement H. Pugsley, *In Sorrow's Lone Hour* (New York: Abingdon Press, 1963), 76.